CRY HAVOC
The History of
War Dogs

CRY HAVOC
The History of War Dogs

Nigel Allsopp

FOREWORD

I have lost count of the number of books I have read on training dogs, together with numerous dog anecdotes, over the past forty years. My keen interest in dogs started in 1970 when I was posted to the United States Army Scout Dog School at Fort Benning, Georgia, USA. I was the first commander of the Explosive Detection Dog Wing at the Army Engineers School of Military Engineering (SME), Moorebank, near Sydney in Australia. I recruited all the dogs and handlers, and commenced training the dogs for service in the War of South Vietnam. In those days we were called the Mine Dog Wing. The engineer mine dog teams did not go to Vietnam because, just as we were packing to go there in 1972, Australia withdrew from the war.

That started a lifetime of fascination about the capabilities and uses of military working dogs. I commenced a military dog breeding program at the SME with technical support from the Commonwealth Scientific Industrial and Research Organisation (CSIRO) on the genetics of our program. We started training the pups in the detection of explosives from the age of three weeks. Every person in my training team of engineer 'doggies' was amazed by the capacity of the dogs to learn new behaviours and search requirements so quickly. We realised that we were only scratching the surface of their capabilities and uses. I needed to know more about the history of military working dogs. There was very little data available to give me an insight into the uses of dogs on a global basis—until now.

Nigel Allsopp has produced a book with an outstanding coverage of the employment of dogs in military and law enforcement agencies around the world. I am amazed that he was able to gain permission to print the material, given the sensitive security nature of dog agencies and their personnel. I use Nigel's book as a point of reference when seeking precedent or researching new ideas. Quite often, I find that what I thought was a 'new' idea has actually been around for a long time somewhere else in the world. This book helps me identify that fact and then provides a point of reference for further information.

For a person who has a love of dogs and an admiration for their uses in military and law enforcement agencies, *Cry Havoc* provides a fascinating insight into the history of dogs and their current-day employment. The information is presented in Nigel's unique way of explanation and this makes it easy to read. Any person who is interested in the use of dogs in roles other than as pets or mascots will find this book a delight.

This book will also galvanise the notion that dogs will be around for a very long time in support of every nation's security interests. The future will continue to hear the call, 'Cry havoc—and let loose the dogs of war!'

George Hulse
Lieutenant Colonel RAE (Retd)
President: Australian Defence Force Trackers and War Dogs Association

ACKNOWLEDGEMENTS

A special thanks to the many embassy defence attaches who have supplied their country's military working dog (MWD) information.

Photographs have been supplied by MWD handlers, both current and retired, by various MWD associations, by official government sources such as embassies, MWD sections and released images from defence websites.

A special thanks to committee members of various international war dog associations who have proofread the chapters pertaining to their country's MWD programs. Also, respective commanding officers from military dog units from the United Kingdom, Australia, United States, Spain, Greece, Sweden, Slovakia, Latvia, Canada, Norway, Singapore and various other countries' servicemen who supplied details.

Finally I would like to acknowledge all the assistance I have had compiling this book; hopefully I have acknowledged you all in the reference section. A special thanks goes to my wife Julie and daughter Jessica who supported my obsession in producing this book. I would also like to point out that since publication I have sadly learnt several dog handlers featured in this book have been killed in action.

CONTENTS

I am a War Dog

High on a hill overlooking the sea,
Stands a statue to honour and glorify me.
Me and my mates that have all gone before,
To help and protect the men of the war.

I am a war dog, I receive no pay,
With my keen, sharp senses, I show the way.
Many of us come from far and around,
Some from death row, some from the pound.

I am a member of the canine pack,
Trained for combat and life on the track.
I serve overseas in those far off lands,
Me and my master working hand in hand.

I lift my head and look across the land,
Beside my master, I await his command.
Together we watch as we wait in the night,
If the enemy comes, we are ready to fight.

In the plantations of Nui Dat I do camp,
The smell print of the VC, to track, as I tramp.
"Seek 'em out boy!" my master does call,
Through the vines of the jungle, together we crawl.

I remember the day we were trapped underground,
With military wildfire exploding all around.
My master and I packin' death through the fight,
Comforting each other till the guns went quiet.

My master's tour of duty has come to an end,
Vietnam he will leave, I will lose a good friend.
No longer will we trudge through the jungles of war,
The canine, the digger, the memory will endure.

Now the years have passed and I patiently wait,
For God to receive me through His celestial gate.
Where I'll roam in comfort for evermore,
He'll keep me safe from the ravages of war.

-Santina Lizzio

INTRODUCTION

The following chapters explore the history of military working dogs (MWDs) throughout the ages, their different roles and the future dogs may have in modern warfare. I have included brief information on civilian police dogs and para-military organisations, though this is an area that could warrant a complete book.

Even though war dogs have been used by man for thousands of years, many of their efforts have escaped public attention. This is highlighted by the lack of dedicated memorials to animal sacrifices in war; most memorials have only been made within the last twenty years. Even today, many returned service organisations do not include a plaque remembering animal deeds. The good news is that this recognition is slowly on the increase and memorials are springing up around the world.

Perhaps today's generation will not accept a military dog serving in combat on operations overseas and being left in theatre or destroyed due to quarantine restrictions preventing its return. Sadly, in the past thousands of animals have been left on the shores of our enemies to unknown fates as we sailed home after the conflicts.

The information in the later part of the book has been supplied by various countries' MWD programs and, as such, many use different terms for handlers or MWD roles. Some of this information also arrived in that country's native language and I only hope I have done service to its translation.

I have commenced this second part of the book with the United Kingdom's Royal Army Veterinary Corps (RAVC). While this unit is not the world's largest user of modern military dogs—it is perhaps behind the USA, France and Russia in this respect—the British do stand out as the world's initiators of the modern war dog for the way they have been used. Many standard roles of military dogs have been developed by the RAVC, partly due to the British Army's regular engagement in conflicts over the last hundred years or so. The RAVC, for example, was practising the art of tracker and patrol dogs in the jungles of Malaysia well before the well-publicised use of dogs in that role by US Forces in Vietnam. Similarly, the RAVC has developed over some 30 years (via the Troubles in Northern Ireland) the use of specialist explosive- and firearms-detection dogs—techniques that can be seen in use today at any vehicle checkpoint in Afghanistan.

I have not included every single country that uses war dogs, but focused on predominant ones and those I have worked with. Some specifics, techniques and names have been deliberately withheld due to ongoing activities and security concerns.

I have based this book in part on my own experiences over some twenty plus years as both a military dog handler and civilian police dog handler. In regards to the history of war dogs, it is, as they say, just yesterday's news. At the time this book is published, new events may have occurred and statistics may have changed.

War Dog Origins

If I describe an animal that has a shared sense of community, is raised by a mated pair with help from other family members, has a dominant hierarchical society, is organised for a hunt and territorial ... I could be talking about man or wolf. No wonder we have shared or competed so much in history.

It is believed by most scientists that the wolf is the ancestor of the domestic dog *Canis familiaris*, which comes in almost every imaginable size and shape, with every possible colour and coat variation. Where did all these varieties come from? Throughout the ages, an amazing number of people have pondered that question. Today, a widely accepted classification of dogs divides them into four main categories (sight hounds, northern group, dingo group and mastiff group), each representing a different origin and sharing certain physical traits. These groups are derived from four of the forty wolf races: *Canis lycaon*, *Canis lupus*, *Canis pallipes* and *Canis lupas chanco*. Some scientists believe the jackal and coyote may have also influenced the domestic dog. It is true that animals in the entire *Canis* group show few differences in terms of anatomy, behaviour or genetics. In fact, all can interbreed and produce fertile offspring, unlike a mating between a horse and donkey which results in an infertile mule.

It is difficult to look at a chihuahua and imagine a wolf at the base of its family tree, but there it is nonetheless. Exactly when and where humans first adopted the wolf into their pack is still subject to debate. Although scientists continue to discuss the evidence, one thing is clear: humans have valued canine companionship for a long time.

About 12,000 years ago, hunter-gatherers in what is now Israel placed a body in a grave with its hand cradling a pup. Whether it was a dog or a wolf can't be known. Either way, the burial is among the earliest evidence of the dog's domestication. Scientists know the process of domestication was underway by about 14,000 years ago but do not agree on why.

The dog's lineage began 37 million years ago in North America, in predators that had distinctive pairs of shearing teeth and ran down prey. Eight million years ago, on what is now the United States Great Plains, a powerful canid, called *epicyon*, the size of a large modern-day wolf, was present. At the same time another canid called *eucyon*, which was fox-size and hunted in packs, was more adaptable as it had teeth suited for eating both meat and plants. The *epicyon* and others of the subfamily Borophaginae followed their large prey into extinction. The adaptable *eucyon* species survived by migrating into the Old World six to four million years ago, eventually evolving into modern canids including wolves, coyotes and jackals. About 800,000 years ago, wolves crossed back to Arctic North America.

From the beginning, the earliest humans may have selected dogs for their abilities such as guarding or hunting. No animal has served man more nobly than dogs in time of conflict. They are a formidable deterrent that is rarely challenged in peace or war.

Dogs make use of all five senses—seeing, hearing, smelling, tasting and touching—to different extents, depending on what they are doing at a particular time. Their olfactory (smelling) and auditory (hearing) senses are particularly acute, and superior to those of humans.

Smell is the dog's most developed sense, far superior to that of the human. This sense is not based on the discrimination of flavours or odours, but on the general classification of smells: useful and useless, friendly and dangerous.

A dog is born deaf and cannot hear until it is approximately 21 days old. The young dog has problems telling what direction sounds come from. Dogs are sensitive to extremely loud noises and high-pitched sound. Some researchers believe a dog's hearing is somewhat more acute than that of a human, able to detect sounds at four times the distance. The dog has a higher range of pitch detection; that is to say, dogs can hear sounds that a human cannot. It also has a superior ability to locate the origin of the sound: a much-desired war dog attribute.

For a long time it was maintained that dogs were mostly colourblind, an opinion that was soundly condemned. It is likely that the external world appears to them in varying highlights of black and gray. A dog sees objects in a wider field (250 degrees) than man. Movement is the type of visual stimulation to which dogs seem very sensitive. If an object is moved, ever so slightly, most dogs will detect it and respond to the movement. Dogs make little use of their eyes in learning, except for their perception of movements. They cannot see as far as humans, but with a lower viewpoint than man, they can detect silhouettes on the horizon sooner. Their low-light vision is better than a human's, due to the predominance of rod receptors in the retina. Night vision is further enhanced by a special reflective layer at the back of the eye called the tapetum.

Man has learnt to use and develop these senses for war. An ancient writer, Camerarius, noted that guard dogs could discriminate Christians from Turks, and a modern authority has stated that dogs employed during World War I could detect men of unfamiliar regiments. Instinctive fidelity and keen scenting power make some dogs particularly suitable for training as an auxiliary in war. A dog also very readily acquires a sense of danger; it was noted during World War I that dogs, if unable to reach or uncertain of a particular destination, would make their way back to their kennels. They would never cross the zone to the enemy.

Although the figures vary depending on who you speak to, I was always taught that my MWD companion (a wolf in disguise) inherited approximately 75 per cent of its knowledge while learnt behaviour accounted for 15 per cent (observing parents) and taught knowledge (training) accounted for less than 10 per cent. Therefore, if all else failed a canine would act on its basic instincts and the four basic responses of fight, flight, feed and reproduction. We harness a lot of these instinctive foundations of temperament to train a war dog: for example, from its sociability instincts we get its courage, protection and combat and from its feeding instinct we get hunting and tracking. If we want a dog to bark we can use its natural behaviour to bark when excited, for example, teasing it with its favourite toy just out of reach. The dog's play drive will cause it to vocalise and we immediately reward the dog for making the noise. The dog will associate the command word you use, or physical action such as a hand gesture, with making a vocal sound, followed by being rewarded (repetition and association). After a while we can make the dog bark on command.

Humans tend to see expression of emotions or actions in animals as a clear sign of their human qualities. This is called 'anthropomorphism'. For those who don't have a dictionary handy, 'anthropomorphism is a term attribution of human characteristics to, a dog or, some would argue recognition of human characteristics in, non-human creatures.'

Given that more than 87 per cent of all US dog owners regard their pet as a member of the family and treat it accordingly, it is not surprising that many people associate their dog's behaviour with human reactions and emotions. No wonder there is such a growing market in dog behaviour specialists telling you what you need (or think you need) to hear. The fact is that dogs need to be dogs, and they act like dogs, not little humans in fur coats. There are usually sound behavioural reasons why dogs do things, most leading back to its basic instincts. For example, some people think that their dog kisses them when they get home. Watch any wolf documentary and see that when the alpha dog and its pack returns from hunting, the pups and omega dog left behind greet the pack by licking the mouth and muzzle. This stimulates a regurgitation reaction in the pack dogs that promptly brings up food for the dogs that had to stay behind.

Does Size Matter?
In the past, dogs were selected predominantly for their size, enabling them to seize a warrior or his horse in battle. Hounds were bred for tracking abilities and the pursuit of escapees, poachers and slaves. Many of the breeds discussed in following chapters will show these same characteristics. During

both world wars, any breed was considered, as well as many crossbreeds (a crossbreed is the progeny of a purebred bitch that has mated with a dog of a different breed) for training. A call for dogs was put out and many pet dogs were offered up for service, due to either poverty or patriotism on behalf of the owner. Some were simply loaned to the Defence Department in the hope that they would survive the war and be returned.

In modern times the process has reverted, with dogs once again selectively bred and developed for the modern battlefield. Today, breeds tend to be standardised due to uniformity within government agencies and the fact that many organisations breed their own dogs and stick to a few types. Most modern war dogs are purebreeds (a purebreed dog is one whose sire and dam are of the same breed; likewise their parents are descendants of the same breed).

Traditionally, the most common breed for police-type operations has been the German shepherd. In recent years there has been a shift to smaller dogs with keener senses of smell for detection work, and more resilient breeds such as the Belgian malinois for patrolling and law enforcement. Most MWDs are paired with a single individual after their training. This person is called a handler. In operational theatres a handler won't stay with one dog for the length of either's career, but only as long as his tour of duty. Due to quarantine requirements, some deployed dogs never return home. In peacetime a handler will usually stay partnered with a dog for his or her career within the 'K-9' mustering.

In the 20th century, it was in Germany that the first great difference of opinion on the most suitable breed for training and military use occurred. Poodles were originally chosen because of their high degree of intelligence, but poodles suffer considerably when exposed to the heat of the sun, and though they have excellent scent abilities, they are extremely shortsighted. The Saint Bernard was then tried. The record of its ancestors at the Great St Bernard Hospice was distinguished enough, but it seemed to have been forgotten that the hospice dog, besides being shorthaired, was also of lighter build than the modern Saint Bernard. The pointer was tried next, but though it has unquestionable intelligence and physical strength, the hunting instinct is so deep-rooted in this breed as to be ineradicable. German authorities had insisted from the outset that 'a military dog cannot be produced from crossbreeds'. During World War I the majority of the dogs employed with the German army were German shepherds. Indeed, according to the returns of the German Society for Ambulance Dogs (Oldenburg), of 1,678 dogs sent to the front up to the end of May 1915, 1,274 were German shepherds, 142 Airedale terriers, 239 Dobermans and 13 Rottweilers. This figure remained proportionate throughout the war.

Over the years, breeds were developed for a variety of reasons. Certain physical traits were cultivated for specific jobs. It is reasonable to say that it is due to man's greater knowledge of genetics, heredity and behaviour that all breeds used by the military today are superior, both physically and mentally, than those of years ago. The main military working dog breeds used today are German shepherds, Dutch shepherds, Dobermans and Rottweilers, while specialist search dogs tend to be labradors and spaniels.

HISTORY OF WAR DOGS

Before the Romans, the Egyptians, Greeks and Babylonians all employed fierce fighting dogs in battle. In Egypt, murals commemorate the fighting spirit of dogs. They show vicious animals unleashed by their soldier-masters leaping upon their feeble enemies. The ancient Egyptian word for dog was *iwiw*, which referred to the dog's bark. They served in hunting, as guard and police dogs and in military actions. Their breed is difficult to discern; paintings show a resemblance to basenji, saluki, greyhounds and mastiffs.

Hammurabi, the sixth king of Babylon who reigned from 1792 to 1750BC, equipped his soldiers with huge war dogs. A war dog was also immortalised in a mural depicting the great Battle of Marathon between the Greeks and Persians.

The Romans had three urban military cohorts, created by Augustus, stationed in Rome itself. Tacitus clearly stated their duty as 'to control the slaves and those citizens whose natural boldness gives way to disorderly conduct, unless they are overawed by force'. The cohorts were regarded part of the imperial army and had considerable power; in effect they were the first Military Police force in history. To carry out their function they employed large, fierce, attack dogs to track down runaway slaves.

In AD 6 Augustus also created the vigiles of 7000 men within the fourteen regions of Rome, who were in effect a cross between firemen and policemen. Their numbers included dog handlers, whose large mastiff-type dogs assisted in putting down riots.

In the Rome legions themselves were specialist staff in the headquarters. One officer post was the *questionarii* (police and investigation staff). This officer had several *immunes*, or legionary soldiers, under his command. The Roman army had no specialist branches but the immunes had an important privilege: immunity from hard labour for soldiers required to undertake special duties. Of interest to us were the *immunes*: *vetinarii* (veterinarians), *victimarii* (men in charge of sacrificial animals), *venatores* (men using dogs to hunt) and *legati propraetor* (governers of military provinces). It was amongst these men that military dog handlers are first mentioned and used in war. Information drawn up by the Romans classified dogs into *canes villatica* (watchdogs), *canes pastorales* (sheepdogs) and *canes vanatici* (hunting dogs). These hunting dogs were further subdivided into *pugnaces* (attackers), *nare sagaces* (trackers) and *pedibus cleres* (chasers). Clearly Romans were using some of the first named military working dogs.

Both Greeks and Romans used dogs for offensive and defensive purposes, and for maintaining communication on the field of battle. War dogs are mentioned by Plutarch and Pliny, and Strabo describes how, in Gaul, dogs were protected with coats of mail. After the fall of Rome, armies across the globe continued using war dogs, but no longer limited their service to fighting. They were trained as guard dogs, sentries, messengers and draught dogs.

Indian dogs were highly prized among the Persian aristocracy. Xerxes I (489–65 BC) reportedly took a large number of them with his army when he marched against Greece. One of the Persian satraps (governers) of Babylon assigned the revenues derived from four large villages in that province to the care of his Indian hounds. A dog belonging to Darius III (336–30 BC) supposedly refused to leave Darius' corpse after he had been struck down by Bessus. The Persian phrase *sag-e karzari* means 'canine warrior'.

During medieval times dog handlers were called *fewterers*. These men were responsible for their lord's war and hunting dogs. They were true military dogs, large mastiff-type breeds trained to attack humans in peace and war (perhaps the first police dogs too). The *fewterers* also trained greyhound-type dogs used for hunting, and hound breeds used as tracker dogs. Medieval knights draped their faithful hounds in chain mail and plunged into battle with the dogs by their side.

Attila the Hun used a pack of large dogs to stand as sentries around his camps, so as not to be surprised by his enemies.

William the Conqueror used St Hubert hounds (bloodhounds) to support his troops as well as to run down opponents. His St Hubert hounds guarded and defended his army's camps and followed remaining enemies to the end of any trail. The Bayeux tapestry shows approximately 623 people, of whom seven are women, as well as 202 horses, 55 dogs, 37 buildings, 41 ships and over 500 amazing mythological creatures. It pictures the events before, during and after the Battle of Hastings in 1066. It is believed some of the dogs are hunting dogs but some are war dogs engaged in the battle itself. A dog collar has been discovered on the battle site: an open-work band of copper alloy backed by leather or velvet, attached to the metal through six small holes.

Edward Longshanks utilised dogs to defend the English Crown in the 13th century. He used armoured dogs to defend caravans or attack enemies, and bloodhounds on his borders with Scotland to track down the notorious 'moss troopers'. Longshanks established tracker dogs in the various districts to assist the Crown forces along the border.

In 1518 King Henry VIII of England presented 400 battle mastiffs, with iron collars, to Charles V of Spain, then at war with France. The Spanish mastiffs were set on the French dogs at the siege of Valencia, and drove them from the field. So heroic was their conduct that Charles held all the dogs up as an example of honour and courage.

In 1599 Queen Elizabeth dispatched the Earl of Essex, Ireland, with an army of 22,000 men, including a large force of 800 bloodhounds, to put down the Irish chieftain rebellion.

The Spanish conquistadors used dogs when they invaded the lands controlled by South American natives.

Dogs were used up until 1770 to guard naval installations in France. In the same period, Frederick the Great used dogs as messengers during the Seven Years War in Russia. Napoleon also used dogs during his campaigns in the early 19th century, unleashing fighting dogs in front of his reserves. After the Battle of Marengo he wrote, 'I walked over the battlefield and saw among the slain, a poodle killed bestowing a last lick upon his dead friend's face. Never had anything on any of my battlefields caused me a like emotion.'

During World War I, the Germans used possibly 30,000 dogs, the French 20,000, and the Italians 3,000. The other Allied forces used thousands more. The French employed *chiens de brie*, large sheep dogs, in sentry duties. In Belgium draught dogs towed gun carriages. Italians used large numbers of dogs in Alpine areas, climbing narrow paths where horses or mules could not venture. Kilo for kilo, a dog can pull a greater weight than a horse. The US did not use war dogs but borrowed some from their Allies.

'Those that hold the lead' is a motto seen on many MWD handlers' t-shirts. The double meaning of the word 'lead' is apt, as MWD handlers are frequently at the forefront of operations. In Vietnam, for example, the dreaded 'walking the point' by infantry soldiers was among the most dangerous of occupations. On many lucky patrols a dog handler was in this position, well forward, awaiting and detecting a Viet Cong ambush.

During offensive operations ranging from World War II to the present Gulf conflicts, mine detection dogs (MDDs) were employed prior to zero hour at the forefront, clearing a path with other engineering assets for the main forces to exploit.

War Dogs Today

The appearance of the ancient warrior with his war dog has not altered greatly over time. The ancient soldier was lightly armed and clad for speed of movement on the battlefield. The war dog wore a light protective jacket made of leather with spikes and matching collar for throat protection at most.

Today, both dog and man are more valued in society and greater protection is afforded to both. Today's war dogs have bulletproof vests and rubber booties for protection. Communication devices and video systems can be attached to the dogs, so handlers can not only see and command dogs in the heat of battle, but also allow them to be recalled to safety if required.

The dog handler is also better clad for battle than ever before, with communications, modern weapons with laser and night vision capabilities, individual night-viewing devices and tactical protective body armour. Handlers also possess a rich knowledge of medical and first aid treatments to immediately aid their canine partners if needed in battle.

Along with wearing advanced equipment, war dogs today are also multi-skilled in battlefield functions. Many are dual-roled to attack or detect specialist substances.

It might be imagined that with the increased complexity of military operations the value of war dogs has declined. In fact, the reverse is true. Dogs still possess many advantages over modern technology and their use is expected to continue well into the future.

Their superior ability to indicate the presence of an intruder up to a kilometre away at night, coupled with their ability to jump fences, cross rivers and apprehend the offender until assistance arrives is formidable. There has never been, or likely going to be, anything capable of replacing them in the future. Dogs are not dependent on a power source; they do not rust up when operating in jungle conditions; nor do they seize up in an Afghanistan sandstorm. When all these attributes are put in one package, the MWD's value is apparent.

Dogs are an invaluable aid to ground troops in jungle warfare, as was demonstrated by the British in the Malayan Campaign and again in Borneo. Additionally, tracker dogs were used by US and Australian forces in Vietnam and, more recently, by Australian troops in East Timor.

Over open country or in urban areas, in pursuit of intruders, detecting enemy forces on patrol or locating terrorist munitions dumps, dogs have been successfully used in Kenya, Cyprus, Hong Kong, Bosnia, Kosovo, Northern Ireland, the Middle East, Asia, Iraq and Afghanistan.

Dogs have been more widely used around the world protecting military installations and vital points. Little wonder that, with the escalation of international terrorism, there has been little abatement in the military's involvement with service dogs.

In modern services, dogs are relatively cost efficient as guard dogs on large military facilities and airfields. A single dog team is capable of covering an area that might otherwise require a platoon. An MWD team is a very effective and efficient force multiplier. With today's fiscal constraints the implications are obvious.

Significant Dates in Military Dog History

628 BC: The Lydians deploy a separate battalion of fighting dogs.

525 BC: The Persian king Cambyses uses huge fighting dogs against Egyptian spearmen and archers.

490 BC: Battle of Marathon: a brave fighting dog is immortalised in a mural.

385 BC: Siege of Mantineia: fighting dogs cut off enemy reinforcements.

210 BC: Hammurabi equips his warriors with huge dogs.

101 BC: Battle of Vercellae: Large kimber dogs led by women defend their *laagers*.

AD 43: Rome invades Britannia. Giant fighting dogs called *pugnaces britanniae* are discovered and exported for integration into the military of ancient Rome.

101: The Romans employ one fighting dog company per legion.

1525: Henry VIII exports 400 mastiffs to support Spain.

1580: Elizabeth I sends 800 fighting dogs to fight in the Desmond Rebellions.

1799: Napoleon assembles large numbers of fighting dogs in front of his reserves.

1915: The Belgian army use carabineers, strong-muscled dogs called *Bouvier des Flandres,* to haul heavy cannons to the front.

1914–1918: Dogs are used by international forces to deliver vital messages.

1941–1945: The Soviet Union uses dogs strapped with explosives to destroy invading German tanks.

1966–1973: Over 4,000 US war dogs serve in the Vietnam War; estimated to have saved over 10,000 human lives.

BREEDS

History has shown many different breeds have been used in the past. These are just a few used by the military today. How true is the adage: 'it's the fight in the dog, not the dog in the fight, that counts'.

One large, ancient breed influenced the use of war dogs throughout history and is commonly considered to be the ancestor of today's mastiff-type dogs. Mastiff-type dogs are often referred to as molossus dogs or molossers. These dogs were used for hunting in ancient Assyria, as well as for military purposes and protection. The ancient mastiffs would later be imported from Assyria, Egypt and Asia Minor. Xerxes I of Persia led predatory wars to enlarge the borders of his empire, taking large war dogs with him. When Sir Peers Legh was wounded in the Battle of Agincourt in 1415, his mastiff stood over and protected him for many hours. Large mastiff breeds have been used by the military for thousands of years. Mastiff types were used to haul supplies during both world wars.

Once the mastiff reached the Roman Empire, it had already been bred to suit special purposes—the first step in the development of 'breeds' within a species. The Roman army had whole companies composed entirely of dogs. They wore spiked collars around their neck and ankles, made more dangerous by the large curved knives protruding from the collars. Sometimes they were starved before battle, then unleashed on an unsuspecting enemy.

The Romans developed one breed that very closely resembles the Swiss mountain dog of today. The Romans took their mastiffs into Gaul, now known as France. The dogs guarded the mountain passes where a few hundred years later the St Bernard would be found. Today, St Bernards are used in Chile by the Mountain Regiment for both search and rescue and patrol work.

These early mastiffs also contributed to French breeds like the *dogue de Bordeaux* and, in Italy, the Neapolitan mastiff. In Spain, very near the homeland of the Great Pyrenees, the Spanish mastiff was developed. To the north, in Belgium, the feared tracker, St Hubert's hound, the ancestor of today's bloodhound, was developed from the descendants of those fierce hunting dogs.

From the Alps, the mastiff is thought to have been adopted by the Germanic peoples and then to have travelled to Great Britain with Angles and Saxons. The great Dane is known as the *Deutsche dogge* (or German mastiff). In AD 43, the Roman conquest of Britain made Britannia a Roman province. At that time in Britain there were giant, wide-mouthed dogs, which the Romans called *pugnaces britanniae*, that surpassed their molossus dogs. A *Procurator Cynegii* was stationed in Venta Belgarum (now Winchester) and responsible for selecting these dogs, which were exported to Rome for contests in the amphitheatre and for use by the Roman army.

The *pugnaces britanniae* were dogs well respected by royalty and warriors. They were given as gifts to men of honour, and many warriors and chiefs took the name as a title to show their loyalty and courage. Hounds were the traditional guardian animals of roads and crossways and are believed to protect and guide lost souls in the Otherworld. The Irish wolfhound was used to hunt wolves and deer, but it was also used as a war dog to attack men on horseback and knock them from their saddles.

The Rottweiler, or *Metzgerhund* (butcher's dog), is a medium- to large-sized breed originating in Germany as a herding dog. Rottweilers worked as draught dogs, pulling carts to carry meat and other products to market. The breed is an ancient one, whose history stretches back again to the Roman Empire. In those times, the legions travelled with their meat on the hoof and required the assistance of working dogs to herd the cattle. One route the army travelled was through Württemberg and on to the small market town of Rottweil. The principal ancestor of the first Rottweilers during this time was supposed to be the Roman droving dog—local dogs the army met on its travels. The Rottweiler was officially recognised in 1910 as a police dog in Germany.

During World Wars I and II, Rottweilers were put into service in various roles, including messenger, draught and guard dogs. Currently, they are often used in search and rescue, assistance, guide dogs for the blind, guard and police dogs in addition to their traditional roles. The Israeli Army considered using them strapped with explosives as suicide dogs as recently as the late 1980s. They are still used by several European military units.

The Airedale was extensively used in World War I to carry messages to soldiers behind enemy lines and to transport mail. They were also used by the Red Cross to find wounded soldiers on the battlefield. There are numerous tales of Airedales delivering their messages despite terrible injury. An Airedale named Jack ran through half a mile of enemy fire with a message attached within his collar. He arrived at headquarters with his jaw broken and one leg badly splintered, and right after he delivered the message, he dropped dead in front of its recipient.

Lt Colonel Edwin Richardson was responsible for the development of messenger and guard dogs in the British Army. The army provided two Airedales (Wolf and Prince) for use as message carriers. After both dogs proved themselves in battle, Airedales were given more duties.

Before the adoption of the German shepherd as the dog of choice for law enforcement, and search and rescue work, the Airedale terrier often filled this role. In 1906, Richardson tried to interest the British police in using dogs to accompany officers, for protection on patrol at night. Airedale terriers were selected for duty as police dogs because of their intelligence, good scenting abilities and their hard, wiry coats that were easy to maintain and clean.

At the beginning of the Russo-Japanese war in 1904, the Russian embassy in London contacted Lt Colonel Richardson for help acquiring dogs for the Russian army, trained to take the wounded away from the battlefields. He sent Airedale terriers, for communication and sanitary services. Although these original imports perished, Airedale terriers were reintroduced to Russia in the early 1920s for use by the Red Army. Special service dog units were created in 1923, and Airedale terriers were used as demolition dogs, guard dogs, police tracking dogs and casualty dogs.

The border collie is a breed of herding dog that originated along the borders of England, Wales and Scotland. It is widely considered to be the most intelligent breed of dog in the world. Because of their skills, border collies make excellent search and rescue dogs in lowland, mountain and urban areas. They have been trained in air-scenting, ground-scenting and as cadaver dogs in many military forces.

Developed in Germany in the late 1800s, the boxer is part of the molosser dog group, a breed of stocky, medium-sized, short-haired dogs. The coat is smooth and fawn or brindled, with or without white markings. Boxers are brachycephalic (they have broad, short skulls) and have a square muzzle, mandibular prognathism (an underbite), very strong jaws and a powerful bite ideal for hanging on to large prey, including man. These strong and intelligent animals have also been used as service dogs, guide dogs for the blind, therapy dogs and in civilian police canine units. The versatility of boxers was recognised early on by the military, where they have been used as valuable messenger dogs, pack carriers, and attack and guard dogs in times of war.

The modern labrador's ancestors originated on the island of Newfoundland, now part of the province of Newfoundland and Labrador, Canada. The breed emerged over time from the St John's water dog, also an ancestor of the Newfoundland dog (to which the labrador is closely related). Labradors are an intelligent breed with a good work ethic and generally good temperaments. Common working roles for labradors include: hunting, tracking and detection (they have a great sense of smell), guide dogs, police and MWDs. An MWD named Sadie, a black labrador, was a 2007 recipient of the Dickin Medal (the animal equivalent of the Victoria Cross).

The spaniel is an old breed, appearing in paintings as early as the 1600s. It is probably the ancestor of most modern spaniels, including springer spaniels and cocker spaniels (who were not recognised as separate breeds until the 1800s). The purpose of the breed was as a hunting dog. Before guns were used to shoot game, the land spaniel would 'spring' or flush the game bird into the air where a trained falcon or hawk would bring it to the handler. The Royal Army Veterinary Corps and US Department of Defense use springer spaniels in various operational theatres. They are ideally suited to explosive and firearm searching, utilising their natural scenting abilities.

Doberman pinschers were first bred by Karl Friedrich Louis Doberman in the town of Apolda, in the German state of Thüringia around 1890, following the Franco-Prussian War. The breed's qualities soon became apparent to both the German police and military who, in World War II, were estimated to have trained more than 200,000 war dogs. The United States Marine Corps also became interested in the Doberman during World War II. The US established seven Doberman war dog platoons. The fourth, fifth, sixth and seventh platoons were sent to the European theatre where they served mostly as sentries. The others were sent to the Pacific, where the first platoon saw incredible action on Bougainville, Guam and Okinawa, and the second and third saw comparably hellish action on Guadalcanal, Kwajalein, Enewetak and Guam. These Dobermans were credited for saving many American lives and they are the official Marine Corps war dog. The Second and Third Marine Platoons on Guam used more war dogs than all other areas of combat in the Pacific.

The bloodhound (also known as the St Hubert hound, first bred in AD 1000 by monks at the St Hubert monastery in Belgium) is a large breed of dog famed for its ability to follow scents hours or even days old over great distances. The combination of keen nose and powerful drive to track give it its place as top scent hound. The breed is used to track escaped prisoners and missing persons, as well as for military use.

The Belgian shepherd dog (malinois) is one of four types considered to be varieties of a single breed rather than as a separate breed. In Belgium, Germany, the Netherlands and other European countries, as well as in the United States, Canada and Australia, the malinois is bred primarily as a working dog for personal protection, detection, police work and search and rescue. The United States Secret Service uses the breed exclusively. The dog is also used extensively by Unit Oketz of the Israel Defense Forces. Oketz favours the slighter build of the malinois to the German shepherd and Rottweiler, which were employed formerly.

The German shepherd dog (also known as an Alsatian), is a breed of large-sized dog that originated in Germany. The German shepherd is a relatively new breed of dog whose origins date to 1899. As part of the herding group, the German shepherd is a working dog developed originally for herding sheep. German shepherds are a very popular selection as working dogs. They are especially well known for their police work, where they are used for tracking criminals, patrolling troubled areas, and detection and holding of suspects. Additionally, thousands of German shepherds have been used by the military. Usually trained for scout duty, they are used to warn soldiers about the presence of enemies, booby traps or other hazards. The German shepherd dog is one of the most widely used breeds in a wide variety of scent-work roles. These include search and rescue, cadaver searching, narcotics detection, explosives detection, accelerant detection and mine detection, among other duties. They are suited for these lines of work because of their keen sense of smell and their ability to work without distraction.

The spitz group of dogs incorporates several breeds used by the military as sledge dogs, commonly called huskies. The Siberian husky, samoyed, and Alaskan malamute are all breeds directly descended from the original sled dog. In this breed of canine, the word 'husky' is a corruption of the derogative term 'Eskie' applied to the Inuit tribes discovered by Europeans who made early expeditions into their lands. Siberian huskies also served in the United States Army's Arctic Search and Rescue Unit of the Air Transport Command during World War II.

The Greenland husky is a rare breed descended from the Arctic wolf with an ancestry over 12,000 years old. They are believed to have been brought to Greenland by the Thule Inuit around AD 1100 and are related to the Inuit dog. The Alaskan husky is not so much a breed of dog as it is a type or a category. It is defined only by its purpose, which is that of a highly efficient sled dog. The Alaskan is the sled dog of choice for world-class dog-sled racing competitions. None of the purebred northern breeds can match it for sheer racing speed. The Alaskan malamute is another member of the spitz group of dogs. It can be traced back 2,000 to 3,000 years to the Mahlemuits tribe of Alaska. Recent DNA analysis shows that malamutes are one of the oldest breeds, genetically distinct from other dogs. Though not scientifically confirmed, the Alaskan malamute may be the closest living relative to the 'first dog'.

There is, of course, no perfect war dog breed. Many a mongrel (meaning a dog or bitch whose sire and dam are likely to owe their make up to any number of different breeds) has served the colours with heroic distinction. Recently in Australia, several crossbreed dogs that had been given a second chance from a dog pound have served in Afghanistan searching for explosives. One of these dogs Sarbi, a black Australian Labrador cross, aged about four was the first army dog to be awarded a prestigious Royal Society for the Prevention of Cruelty to Animals' Purple Cross for exceptional service to humans. Many crossbreed dogs have made the ultimate sacrifice.

ROLES OF MILITARY WORKING DOGS

Over the centuries dogs have had many roles with the military. While in the past they have done everything from catch rats to draw fire to expose enemy positions, today dogs are given humane tasks where their special skills do the most good.

Why have we used dogs in war? In addition to the fine qualities dogs offer as team members, their visual and olfactory sensory abilities are literally superior to ours. They can go where a soldier cannot and can often subdue or intimidate a foe more quickly with non-lethal force if required.

Among the dog's abilities that far exceed a man's is its sense of smell. Dogs are reported to have ten to twenty times the number of receptors in their nose compared with a human, and the olfactory part of their brain is proportonally much larger. This gives them the ability to detect very faint odours and to discriminate between very slight differences in chemical composition. Dogs rely on their sense of smell in much the same way humans rely on their eyesight. This makes them ideal for tasks such as tracking, detection of explosives or narcotics, casualty location, and search and rescue. In the right environment a dog can detect intruders up to 1000 metres away.

Guard and Police Dogs
Guard dogs were the most commonly used military dogs prior to the advent of a role change to military working dogs (MWDs) by most services. Guard dogs were trained like civilian police dogs and used to defend military facilities, usually operating at night. They announce the presence of prowlers

and can be released off their leash to both bite and hold, or bail up a suspect until the handler arrives.

These dogs have been used to guard nuclear weapons storage sites and military airfields. During the Vietnam War, the United States Air Force police employed dog teams as perimeter protection prior to Viet Cong attack. Today, guard and attack dogs are used to patrol perimeters of bases in Afghanistan, much as they first did in the trenches during World War I.

Combat Scout Dogs and Tracker Dogs

Since early times humans have taken advantage of the keen scenting powers of dogs to search for lost or fugitive persons. English soldiers used tracking hounds in the 1600s to follow the trail of highwaymen who fled justice in unsettled rural parts of the country. In the United States, tracking hounds were used to follow runaway slaves before the Civil War. More recently these dogs were trained to silently locate booby traps and concealed enemy troops. Scout dogs were used in World War II, Korea, the Vietnam War, NATO Operations, Iraq, Afghanistan, and current operations in Israel, to name a few. With all the modern technology such as night vision equipment, radars and other detection devices in service, an MWD is still the most effective way to conduct a forward patrol in either rural or urban environments. During the Vietnam War labradors were used to track enemies and locate lost or missing troops. These dogs were often used for re-establishing contact with the Viet Cong and also to reconnoitre the area for possible Viet Cong activity. The combat tracker teams were assigned to a larger platoon but often travelled far in front to maintain noise integrity.

Mine Detecting Dogs

In World War II the US mine detecting dogs (MDDs) were trained by negative reinforcement. Underground wires shocked the dogs, teaching them that danger lurked under the dirt. Once the dog's focus was properly directed, dummy mines were planted and the dogs were trained to signal their presence. Due to the stress this caused, dogs could only work for 20 or 30 minutes at a time.

Fortunately, the British trained their dogs using the trusted method of praise and reward after scent recognition and their dogs were far more effective. A single MDD team can clear an area the size of a football field in under an hour, whereas a man would take all day. The MDD field has grown in step with humanitarian concerns. The national dog program in Afghanistan has been very successful, with more than 130 dogs and handlers operating in the field. MDDs in Bosnia and Herzegovina have quickly established themselves as an important part of mine detection operations, mainly due to the speed at which they can 'proof' (clear) an area.

Explosive detection dogs (EDDs) are trained to detect all types of anti-personnel and anti-tank mines. In combat zones the process is referred to as 'mine clearance'. The priority is to breach the minefield quickly to create a safe path for troops. In times of relative peace, the process of mine removal is referred to as 'demining'. 100 million mines laid in the world do not discriminate between combatants and non-combatants, and are responsible for killing or maiming hundreds of people every day.

A dog is trained to indicate the presence of an explosive by calmly sitting a short distance from the location where the scent was discovered. When any dog indicates, the location is marked on the edges of the task area. If this is the first dog, another dog will traverse the area up to the indicated location again. Manual deminers can safely approach the location across ground that has been cleared by both dogs. The dogs work best in clear open country with vegetation no higher than calf to knee height (depending on vegetation and dog abilities). In Afghanistan, dogs are not used in wet conditions, thick vegetation or residential areas where, it is thought, the profusion of strong scents is likely to confuse the dogs.

Messenger Dogs

Dogs had a vital part to play in World War I as the complexes of trench warfare throughout the Western Front meant that communication was always a problem. Communication systems were crude, and there was a very real possibility that vital messages from the front would never get back to headquarters. Dogs proved to be as reliable as soldiers in the dangerous job of running messages across dangerous ground back to headquarters. Some units used two dog handlers with whom the dog had rapport and it would run from one to the other. The more common method was employing a handler with several dogs. He would dispatch a dog forward with an allied soldier who, when required, would place a message in a tube attached to the collar of the dog and release him back to his master. The dog would be fed on its return as a reward. The danger of this method was the possibility of allied troops feeding and caring for the dogs, who then stayed with them in the trenches.

Sentry Dogs

In one of their earliest military uses, sentry dogs were used to defend camps or other priority areas at night and sometimes during the day. They would bark or growl to alert civilian or military guards of a stranger's presence. During the Cold War, the US military used sentry dog teams outside nuclear weapons storage areas.

A test program was launched in Vietnam two days after a successful Viet Cong attack (1 July, 1965) on Da Nang air base. Forty dog teams were deployed to Vietnam. The teams were placed on the perimeter in front of machine gun towers and bunkers. The detection of intruders resulted in a rapid deployment of reinforcements. The test was successful. Handlers returned to the US and dogs were reassigned to new handlers. The air force immediately started to ship dog teams to all the US bases in Vietnam and Thailand.

Anti-Tank Dogs

During World War II, the Soviet Union trained anti-tank dogs. Whenever these dogs were fed it was under a hull of a tank, so an association between food and a tank soon developed. They were then starved prior to battle and, when released, would run under a German tank to seek food. The dogs wore a kind of pouched, canvas overcoat, similar to a modern dog warmer, in which high explosives or a magnetic mine was placed. When the dog ran under the tank the explosives were activated. Reports indicate some 300 German tanks were destroyed this way.

Attack Dogs

In ancient times dogs, usually large mastiff and Rottweiler-type breeds, would be strapped with armour and spiked collars, and sent into battle to attack the enemy. The dogs were taught to attack chariots, men and cavalry by biting at the horses' fetlocks, and to attack other dogs used by the enemy.

This approach has been largely abandoned in modern-day militaries, due to the fact that modern weapons would allow the dogs to be destroyed almost immediately. In Okinawa, US soldiers quickly eliminated a platoon of Japanese soldiers and their dogs. The British army did employ compound dogs in the Far East in the 1950s to '70s, where aggressive dogs were let loose at night in a warehouse or ammunition dump. If anyone broke in, a duty member of the Royal Army Veterinary Corps would attend to call the dogs off—assuming the offender was still in one piece.

The East German border guards used dog runs (*Kettenlaufanlagen*), which were installed on high-risk sectors of the border. The dogs generally were chained to steel cables up to 100 metres (330 ft) long. The dogs were occasionally turned loose in temporary pens adjoining gates or damaged sections of the fence. By the 1970s, there were 315 dog runs with 460 dogs. This figure increased steadily until a total length of 71.5 kilometres (44.4 miles) of dog runs had been installed by mid-1989, and 2,500 dogs employed.

Haulage Dogs

Around the time World War I broke out, Europeans often used dogs to pull small carts. Many European armies adapted the process for military use. The Belgian army used dogs to pull their maxim guns. These guns were too small for horses to pull and dogs were found to be ideal; relatively speaking a dog is twice as strong as a horse. Mastiffs could pull up to 220 kilograms (500 pounds) each in a wheeled cart: this could include carrying supplies or wounded soldiers. The French employed 250 dogs at the start of World War I in this role. The Dutch Army copied the idea and had hundreds of dogs trained and ready by the end of World War I (the Netherlands remained neutral). This practice was still being used by the British Expeditionary Force (BEF) of the Eastern Command in World War II, where light haulage dogs carried ammunition. Pack dogs were used when there was not enough snow on the ground to operate a toboggan or the terrain was too dense, such as in forested areas. The Soviet army also used dogs to drag wounded men to aid stations during World War II. These dogs were well-suited to transporting loads over snow and through craters. Today the Colombian army uses pack dogs to carry light loads such as ammunition and medical supplies. Search and rescue dogs often carry water or first aid supplies for when they locate a victim.

Sledge dogs have been used for thousands of years by indigenous people to haul supplies. During World War II the Americans used sled dog teams for rescue work; teams were also engaged in freighting, communication work and other routine operations. But everything was dropped when a sudden call came through for a special mission. The German army was making its last great breakthrough in December 1944 and Von Runstedt's army rolled through the Ardennes. American aviation was grounded by impossible flying conditions, while the Panzer armies drove on through bitter cold and heavy snow that rivalled even the Arctic. Lives were lost due to the delays in bringing wounded back from the front lines to advance medical stations. It was General Patton who came up with the idea of using husky teams.

Teams and their drivers had been stationed at widely distant points over the Arctic Circle so that they could rapidly reach crippled planes wherever they crashed. The order went out for 23 picked teams to be collected by C-47s from remote stations in Greenland, Labrador, Newfoundland and other points in Canada. Four days after the movement orders reached the Arctic stations, the first planeload of dogs and drivers landed at Toul, France. Clearing weather and the retreat of the German attack kept the teams from showing their full ability, but the operation had set a remarkable record.

The Americans, although they did not use dogs themselves in World War I, supplied over 400 dogs suitable for alpine operations to the French Army. Dog teams operating in the mountainous region could transport up to ninety tonnes of artillery ammunition in four days; the same amount took mules, men and horses over two weeks. Italy used dog teams in the mountain for the transportation of materials and medical evacuation of the wounded.

Dogs were also credited with ambush detection when encountering Austrian troops. In mountainous terrain, Italian dogs usually operated in teams of three, the lead dog in the centre. Dog handlers in the Italian alpine forces were called *Cagnari*. Italy used local shepherd breeds and around 250 were trained at the Military Kennels at Bologna. Dogs had to be 10 months to three years old, white with heavy coats.

Although the US army had used sled dogs in Alaska as far back as the 1900s, drivers had been hired civilians on contract. The 10th Mountain Division was started in World War II in fort Lewis Washington, then sent to Camp Hale, Colorado, in 1942. This unit included dogsled drivers on initial establishment. The concept was that these teams would be used for resupply during a proposed invasion of Norway. With the increasing presence of the military in Alaska during World War II, the USAF 10th Air Rescue Squadron operated up to 200 dogs. The modus operandi was to rescue downed Soviet pilots who were flying lead lease aircraft from Alaska to Siberia. During World War II sledge dog teams were also used in Greenland in patrol and surveillance operations against the Germans. Sled dogs are still used today by several armed forces.

Casualty Dogs

Casualty dogs are perhaps one of the oldest types of military dog. The ancient Greek army used dogs to lick wounds clean after battle. It was believed dog saliva processed a type of mild antiseptic and helped to prevent infection. Casualty dogs, like search and rescue dogs, are trained to indicate casualties lying in obscure places that are difficult for collecting parties to locate. In cases of severe shock or haemorrhage, minutes saved in locating such casualties often meant the difference between life and death.

The Red Cross dogs were by far the most organised and successful canine unit in this field during World War I. The dogs carried medical supplies and canteens to wounded soldiers. They were trained to ignore dead soldiers. If a soldier was found unconscious, the dogs would return to their handlers and lead them to the soldier. Red Cross dogs often worked at night and relied on their olfactory abilities to find soldiers. This type of dog is more likely to be used today by para-military organisations.

Tunnel Dogs

In Vietnam there was a specialised requirement for tunnel dogs to detect and flush out the Viet Cong. The Viet Cong feared dogs and used tactics to try to confuse them, such as washing with US army soap and covering air vents with shirts taken from Americans so the dogs' sense of smell would not be alerted.

Specialist Narcotic and Explosives Detection Dogs

Narcotic detection dogs (NDDs) are usually operated by Military Police units. Specialist MWDs provide an invaluable service in the war on drugs, able to detect illegal substances.

Dogs trained in drug detection are normally used at airfields, border crossing entry points and other places where there is a need for anti-contraband measures. In peacetime drug dogs are used by Military Police to prevent service personnel using illegal substances and creating dangerous workplace environments.

Both MWDs and their civilian counterparts provide an invaluable service in the war on drugs, sniffing out a broad range of narcotics despite efforts at concealment. Provided they have been trained to detect it, MWDs can smell small traces of nearly any illegal substance, even if it is in a sealed container.

MWDs are perhaps at their most valuable when they are trained to detect explosives. Just as with narcotics, trained MWDs can detect minuscule amounts of a wide range of explosives. These dogs are capable of achieving over 98 per cent success rate in bomb detection. They are also in demand for patrolling ahead of troops on the roadside where suspect improvised explosive devices (IEDs) may be present.

Few other criminal acts create such concern and fear in the hearts of a nation's citizens as a series of bombings. It is no coincidence that organised crime and terrorist groups routinely use explosive materials as a means of achieving their violent goals. Whether the objective is murder, intimidation, extortion or governmental disruption, the bomb is a favourite and effective weapon of the criminal element. One of the most effective countermeasures to the use of explosives is the deterrent value and the detection capabilities of the EDD team. EDD teams fill distinctive roles in Military Police operations in addition to their routine use as patrol dog teams.

Public knowledge that EDD teams are assigned to and are used at an installation acts as a deterrent to persons who may try to use explosives illegally. The knowledge that explosives can be detected by EDDs at installation gates or in places where explosives have been hidden can prevent a person from attempting to bring explosives onto an installation.

PRISONER OF WAR HANDLING

One of the basic principles of gaining control over enemy prisoners after capture is to retain the shock of the event. This enables enemy prisoners to be interviewed by intelligence officers seeking vital information. Military working dogs are effectively used to guard and intimidate masses of prisoners, a role that would otherwise require high manpower levels.

The use of war dogs on prisoners by the United States in the context of its recent wars in Afghanistan and Iraq has been very controversial. The United States has used dogs to intimidate prisoners in Abu Ghraib prison. Even prior to this recent event, guard dogs have suffered from images of World War II German dogs attacking concentration camp victims.

In a Peacetime Environment

In peacetime military working dog (MWD) teams are predominantly used to support a variety of Military Police operations. MWD teams can prove an additional asset for security measures, helping Military Police deter and detect the enemy.

All of the MWD employment concepts revolve around the basic skills of the army patrol dog. Some patrol dogs may subsequently be trained in additional skills, such as tracking, narcotics detection and explosives detection.

The decision to employ patrol dogs must be weighed carefully by the responsible commander to ensure that, if patrol dog teams are committed, all lesser means of force have been reasonably attempted. The patrol dog is trained to detect personnel, pursue, attack and hold any intruder who attempts to avoid apprehension or escapes from custody. Releasing the dog constitutes the conscious application of physical force. Patrol dogs may be released to apprehend an intruder who is suspected of committing a serious offence and tries to escape or use deadly force.

The primary function of a patrol dog team on a fixed post is surveillance over an area or building. If used outside, the team is located downwind where the dog can detect an intruder by scent. If this is not possible, the team is located so an intruder can be detected by sight and sound. The patrol dog's contribution to the law enforcement effort is most effective when the team is used on foot patrol. A walking patrol can check or clear buildings and patrol parking lots, family housing areas and troop billet areas. Patrol dog teams are also used to escort and safeguard funds.

Riot control, crowd control and public safety response are just a few names given to police or military squads controlling a large group of demonstrators. High-ranking commissioned officers are usually required to authorise the use of MWDs at a riot. The service dog can be employed to attack armed aggressors who try to hide in the crowd. In such cases the employment of a service dog provides the on-site commander with an additional step in the escalation of force that ranges from the use of batons to the use of firearms.

SPECIAL FORCES CANINE TEAMS

In World War II many military working dog (MWD) handlers were regarded as rear echelon troops assigned to guard railways, ammunition dumps, military bases and prisoners of war (POWs). In more recent time the roles have developed from semi-static guard patrols to specialist search MWDs and forward scouting and tracker tasks. In recent wars MWD handlers find themselves not only in the front line, but usually leading the front line units.

Special forces have had an on/off relationship with military working dogs. They were among the pioneers in their use as patrol and scout dogs, parachuting teams well behind enemy lines to help detect German patrols in World War II. The British Parachute Regiment has had a long association with military dogs. Para dogs jumped during the European invasion and at Arnhem.

The Royal Army Veterinary Corps trained New Zealand Special Air Service troopers as tracker dog handlers in Malaysia to hunt down Communist terrorists during the 1950s. During the Cold War, far from being regarded as secondary troops, MWDs were more likely to face elite opponents, such as Russian *Speznatz*. Many countries enhanced their MWD handlers' training to match this status. MWD handlers today have themselves evolved to be efficient infantry soldiers, well versed in combat skills and with high fitness levels.

Nearly every Special Operation Forces (SOF) mission can benefit from the inclusion of dogs, particularly in support of operations conducted in developing countries that cannot employ or sustain complex and technologically sophisticated equipment.

Yet special forces have to train actively to counter and kill enemy MWDs and practise escape and evasion drills from tracker dog teams. During operations in the Mekong Delta area, Vietnam, the US Navy SEAL teams had to develop a stainless steel pistol called the hush puppy, purposely designed to eliminate Viet Cong sentry dogs. The Smith and Wesson model 39 (modified) had a shoulder stock, a locking slide and a suppressor. (The slide locked for maximum noise reduction and its suppressor limited the effective range to around 100 yards.) Only a few hundred were made, and they were mainly used for disabling sentries, killing guard dogs and shattering lights.

A recent report stated that an amazing tactic has been devised to cut down the United Kingdom's Special Air Service regiment's soaring casualty rates. Fearless MWDs are being trained to jump from aircraft at 7,000 metres (25,000 feet) wearing their own oxygen masks and strapped to special forces assault team members. Once down in hostile terrain in Iraq or Afghanistan, the dogs will be sent in first to seek out insurgents' hideouts, with tiny cameras fixed to their heads. The cameras beam live TV pictures back to the troops, warning of ambushes or showing enemy leaders' locations.

An SAS source said: 'The dogs will be exposed to very high levels of danger on these operations and you never know what's going to be behind a door. Nobody wants to see the dogs get killed but if it's their life or a man's it is obvious which the CO would prefer.'

The dogs will be used in a highly skilled technique called 'high altitude high opening', jumping as much as 32 kilomteres (20 miles) from their targets and gliding towards them for up to 30 minutes. Two have been issued to each of the regiment's four squadrons and troopers have been specially selected to be their handlers.

ARMOURED PROTECTION FOR MILITARY WORKING DOGS

With an increase in roadside bombings and suicide incidents in current operations, the need for armoured protection has also increased. Likewise, the terrorist modus operandi in current conflicts has shown that support and rear echelon forces are equally vulnerable to attack. Military working dogs (MWDs) worldwide are finding an ever-increasing role in protecting these facilities, VIPs and support structures, as terrorists see these as weak and easy targets. Increasingly MWDs are placed in harm's way to protect the potential targets and must be likewise protected with armoured vehicles.

The current role of the MWD teams includes searches at vehicle checkpoints or conducting search and seizure operations well into hostile held territory, which require better protection than soft skin vehicles as transport. In many cases it appears the tradition of transporting a MWD team is to simply throw them in the back of an armoured vehicle with other troops who are heading in the same direction.

Few countries have provided specialist canine vehicles with armoured protection. Yet, in peacetime, many police and military units do provide custom-built dog vehicles with ventilation, separation cages and storage facilities to house this vital asset. In fact many state and national laws as well as animal welfare and humane societies require dogs to be transported in a safe manner. So why don't we comply with this same approach in a war zone?

Although many units deploy their dog teams in armoured vehicles to and from the operational areas, these vehicles are not constructed to cater for the needs of a MWD. Dogs require air-conditioning and ventilation systems in countries such as Iraq, where temperatures can soar up to 60°C (145°F). When the dogs are hot, they tire quickly and their ability to detect explosives and other dangers is greatly reduced. Storage areas for specialist kit can act as a kennel while the dog is on downtime between searches.

The Israeli military dog unit and border police canine teams have specialist dog vehicles; however they lack total ballistic protection for their valuable cargo. If you consider many agencies cost a fully operational dog at around $50,000 each, there could be $300,000 in the six cages of a $30,000 vehicle! It makes fiscal sense to protect this outlay. In peacetime, Military Police units tend to have specialist vehicles similar to their civilian counterparts with air-conditioned pods. Sedan vehicles used by Military Police during garrison duty such as patrolling airfields and military camps are not suitable to operational environments.

Dog Memorials

The glamour gone, some scattered graves and memories dim remain
With their old pals across a field, they'll never trek again
But yet there's nothing they regret as they await their call
For what was done or lost or won, they did their bit – that's all

Now as silent as the guns have fallen
Their tired hearts resting, closed eyes of loving grace
I ask in your quiet thoughts of Honourable Remembrance
You allow them, the animals to take their long awaited place.

Please in the silence of the hour spare some thought for this forgotten Army.

Memorials have always been the virtues against which soldiers are measured. For his distinguishing qualities, a soldier is given medals and the recognition of his country. Military working dogs (MWDs) also possess these qualities. Man's best friend has faithfully served in wars for thousands of years as scouts, sentries, messengers and much more They have served in many conflicts without compensation or recognition, and have not been honoured for their sacrifice. These gallant dogs have more than earned the right to be fully recognised for their service to their countries.

For decades, US veteran dogs deemed too old to serve (ten years and older) were euthanised. Thanks to a law passed in 2000, retired military dogs can now be adopted by their current or former handlers, law enforcement agencies, or individuals capable of caring for them. For many years there was no national memorial to recognise the profound contributions of war dogs to the US military. That has been corrected, largely through the efforts of the Vietnam Dog Handler Association.

One of the earliest recorded memorials to dogs was after the battle between rival Greek states in the Peloponnesian War, 431–404 BC. The Corinthians used guard dogs as shoreline sentries as defence against the Athenian flotilla. According to legend, 50 war dogs leaped with open jaws at the Athenians as they crept ashore on a surprise night-time attack. The dogs fought ferociously but were all slain, bar one who awoke the Corinthians troops in a nearby town by barking. The Corinthians rallied and defeated the Athenians. So grateful were they that they built a monument to honour the dogs. Sorter, the surviving dog, was awarded a special collar inscribed 'Defender and Savior of Corinth'.

Following World War I, a public memorial building was erected at Kilburn, England honouring war dogs. Its inscription reads in part 'This building is dedicated as a memorial to the countless thousands of God's humble creatures who suffered and perished in the Great War of 1914-1918 knowing nothing of the cause but looking forward to final victory, filled with only love, faith and loyalty, they endured much and died for us.' In 1918 a bronze statue of a German shepherd mounted upon a three-mere (ten-foot) granite monument was built in Hartsdale, New York, to commemorate the bravery of dogs in war.

The United States, thanks primarily to many motivated veteran handlers, has been instrumental in establishing war dog memorials. The proposed National War Dog Monument will be erected in the greater Washington DC area. It will proudly honour all military working dogs who have served their country for the last century and into the future. The inscription will read 'In perpetual honour of the service and sacrifice of all military working dogs of all armed services of all wars and peacekeeping missions since World War I.'

On 21 July 1994, a memorial was dedicated at the US Marine Corps war dog cemetery on Guam to honour the dogs who served in the Pacific theatre during World War II. In the battle for Guam (21 July to 10 August 1944) a Doberman named Kurt saved the lives of 250 Marines when he warned them of Japanese troops ahead. Kurt is honoured by a life-sized bronze and granite statue at the memorial on Guam. Carved into the stone are names of twenty-five other Dobermans who gave their lives liberating the island and who are buried nearby. An exact replica of this memorial is located at the University of Tennessee College of Veterinary Medicine.

More than 1,000 dogs had trained as Marine Devil Dogs during World War II. Rolo, one of the first to join the Devil Dogs, was the first Marine dog to be killed in action. Twenty-nine war dogs were listed as killed in action; 25 of those deaths occurred on the island of Guam. The first Marine dog platoon with twenty-four Dobermans and German shepherds landed on Bougainville on 1 November, 1943, moving ahead of the main body of men, looking for snipers in the jungle. Six dogs were recognised for heroism on Bougainville, with the Second and Third Marine Raider Battalions.

Alabama's MWDs and their handlers had their day recently at the dedication of the Alabama War Dogs Memorial at USS *Alabama* Battleship Memorial Park. The memorial depicts the Alabama war dog team of Little Joe, a German shepherd, his handler, Charles 'Wade' Franks, and other combat patrol riflemen. Little Joe gave his life for those men on 22 February, 1970, in Vietnam. The Alabama War Dog Memorial Foundation plans a service dog retirement centre as well. The four-tonne granite slab supports statues depicting a war dog, his handler and other soldiers. The marble slab lists war dogs associated with handlers from Alabama. In front of the piece are boot prints made from an actual soldier's footwear, along with paw prints.

On 21 February, 2000, the first official war dog memorial was unveiled at March Field Air Museum in Riverside, California and an identical second memorial was dedicated 8 October, 2000 (Columbus Day) at the National Infantry Museum, Fort Benning, Columbus, Georgia. Dog teams trained at Fort Benning before serving in Korea and Vietnam. Dog teams are credited with reducing casualties by 65 per cent in Korea alone. The memorial is a special place for dog handlers where they can gather to remember their dogs, their buddies and their missions, or just look back to celebrate the heritage and history of war dogs. The inscription reads: 'They protected us on the field of battle. They watch over our eternal rest. We are grateful.'

Although the British were among the pioneers of war dog use, it was not until 2004 that a memorial dedicated to animals in war was unveiled. The Animals in War memorial is located at Brook Gate, Park Lane, on the edge of London's Hyde Park. Unveiled on 24 November, 2004 by the Princess Royal, it exists as a memorial to the huge number of animals that have served and died under British military command throughout history.

On a smaller scale than memorials, some units have devised medals to honour their combat hero dogs. The Dickin Medal was instituted in 1943 by Maria Dickin to honour the work of animals in war. It is a large bronze medallion, bearing the words 'For Gallantry' and 'We Also Serve' within a laurel wreath, carried on a ribbon of striped green, dark brown and pale blue. Traditionally, the medal is presented by the Lord Mayor of the City of London. It has become recognised as 'the animal's Victoria Cross'. By 2008, it had been awarded 26 times to service dogs. Some examples of the award in the modern era are:

• 2000: Gander – A special one-off posthumous Dickin Medal award was made in 2000 to a Canadian dog named Gander for actions in 1941 which would have been honoured at the time, had the PDSA been informed.

• 2002: Salty and Roselle – guide dogs who separately led their owners to safety from the World Trade Centre during the 11 September 2001 terrorist attacks.

• 2002: Apollo – a search and rescue dog with the New York Police Department, as a representative of all such dogs who worked at the World Trade Centre site and the Pentagon in the aftermath of the 11 September 2001 terrorist attacks.

• 2003: Sam – a Royal Army Veterinary Corps dog serving with The Royal Canadian Regiment in Bosnia-Herzegovina, for separately disarming a gunman and later holding back a hostile crowd while guarding a refugee compound until reinforcements arrived.

• 2003: Buster – a Royal Army Veterinary Corps arms and explosives search dog serving with the Duke of Wellington's Regiment in Iraq, for finding an extremist group's hidden arsenal of weapons and explosives.

• 2007: Sadie – a black labrador retriever was awarded the medal for finding a bomb planted underneath sandbags, close to where a German soldier was killed by a suicide car bombing outside the United Nations headquarters in Kabul in November 2005. Sadie became the 25th canine recipient of the medal, which she received from Her Royal Highness Princess Alexandra. Sadie served in Bosnia, Iraq and Afghanistan and is part of the 102 Military Working Dog Support Unit of the Royal Army Veterinary Corps based in Sennelager, Germany.

• 2009: HRH Princess Alexandra awarded black labrador Treo the Dickin Medal at the Imperial War Museum in London. The now retired dog, from 104 Military Working Dog Support Unit, North Luffenham barracks in Rutland, twice found hidden bombs in Helmand province.

• A total of 25 other dogs, 32 World War II messenger pigeons, three horses and one cat have won the award.

Just as private donations have produced several unofficial war memorials, individuals or groups have also awarded medals to dogs. During the summer of 1917, Stubby, a stray pit bull picked up from the streets of Hartford, Connecticut, by Private J. Robert Conroy, became the mascot of the 102nd Infantry, part of the army's 26th Yankee Division. Stubby served 18 months 'over there' and participated in seventeen battles on the Western Front. He saved his regiment from surprise mustard gas attacks, located and comforted the wounded, and caught a German spy. General John Pershing, who commanded the American Expeditionary Forces during the war, presented Stubby with a gold medal made by the Humane Society and declared him a 'hero of the highest calibre'.

In 2008 some of Australia's unsung military heroes have finally been recognised for their bravery. For the first time, unofficial medals have been awarded to the country's courageous canines by the Australian Defence Force Trackers and War Dogs Association (ADFTWDA). In September 2007, explosive detection dog Razz was working in Afghanistan when he found a large roadside bomb. He moved his sit position and the device was detonated moments before Australian troops moved in to try to defuse it. His handler stated it was a huge bomb and poor Razz was vaporised. Razz not only saved his handler's life but the lives of the troops around him. Six medals, two of them posthumous, were presented to explosive detection dog (EDD) teams of two Combat Engineers Regiment at a ceremony at Brisbane's army barracks.

Another EDD called Aussie was awarded two medals for both operational service and for his five years of service in the Australian Defence Forces. The eight-year-old golden retriever, who has served in Afghanistan and the Solomon Islands, was one of six dogs to receive the medals during a ceremony at the army barracks. In 2008 the army lost three explosives detection dogs on active duty in Afghanistan. On the 5 April 2011, An Australian Military Working Dog called Sarbi was awarded an RSPCA Purple Cross Award at the Australian War Memorial. The Australian Special Forces Explosive Detections dog was declared missing in action September 2008 following a battle with the Taliban which left nine soldiers wounded, including her handler. Sarbi was missing for 13 months, before she was reunited with her handler after being spotted wandering with an Afghan man in north-eastern Oruzgan Province. During her time alone in Afghanistan, Sarbi showed an incredible resilience and strength. And it is her courage and her unquestioning, unwavering service to man that has seen her recognised for a Purple Cross. Sadly, again in June 2010, Sapper Darren Smith and EDD, Herbie, were killed in action.

The ADFTWDA issues two unofficial canine medals:

(1) The War Dog Operational Medal. This is issued to those military working dogs who have served for a minimum period of twenty-eight days in a theatre or war or an area of operations.

(2) The Canine Service Medal. This is issued to those working dogs who have served for a continuous period of five years.

In the Australian Defence Force both the Army and the RAAF have MWD teams. Both the Royal Australian Corps of Military Police (RACMP) and the RAAF, like their EDD counterparts from the Combat Engineer Regiment have received medals for operational duties. Since the raising of the unit, four MPDs have made the ultimate sacrifice. A memorial was held for MPD Ziggy in Camp Phoenix, East Timor where his ashes are interred. The ADFTWDA has also awarded medals to service dogs from the police, corrective services and other government agencies.

The United States House of Representatives approved a House Resolution in March 2010, introduced by Congressman Leonard Lance (NJ-07) honouring MWDs of the United States for their service throughout that nation's history.

'Throughout our nation's history military working dogs have made great contributions to help our military men and women accomplish their important missions,' Lance said during a speech on the House floor. 'These dogs have helped save lives and protect our soldiers in harm's way'.

Specifically, Lance's resolution recognises the significant contributions of the MWD program to the United States armed forces, honours active and retired military working dogs for their loyal service, and supports the adoption and care of these quality animals after their service. Lance said for more than six decades MWDs have helped prevent injuries and saved the lives of thousands of Americans.

There are many more private or regional memorials to war dogs across the world. The bond of affection for these dogs will no doubt give rise to more over the years. Military canines make contributions every day while they serve in our military. They are hard working and do a great job of saving the lives of their handlers and the troops who walk in their footsteps. There has been many a dog handler who has turned to his dog in the depths of war and told him things he would never say to another soldier. MWDs have been a source of friendship, family and true love to their handlers—the price they ask is a pat and a smile. While we often focus on the human cost of operations we must never forget the ultimate sacrifice made by man's best friend.

MASCOTS AND CANINE COMPANIONS

There are several complete books on the subject of military mascots, so I will only briefly explore them in this chapter. They have been of great moral value to soldiers from the trenches of World War I to dogs adopted by Coalition Forces in Afghanistan today.

Dogs are steadfast and loyal, and it is these traits, along with their devotion and courage, that has caused man to seek their companionship in time of war. Many of these dog mascots have received the highest awards for bravery in battle. Unlike their military working dog (MWD) counterparts, they do not actively fight alongside their masters but equally they provide moral and comfort to troops during adverse conditions.

There are two types of military mascots. Those who appear, particularly in Commonwealth forces, as part of the regiment's official history are part of the order of battle with service rank and number. 'Official' British army mascots are entitled to the services of the Royal Army Veterinary Corps, as well as quartering and feeding at public expense. There are also mascots whose costs are borne by the regiment or unit itself.

The Irish wolfhound, for example, is the mascot of the Irish Guards. The first one was given to the regiment in 1902 and they were kept as pets until they became the official mascots in 1961. Although fearsome looking, wolfhounds are generally good natured and well behaved. They thus make perfect regimental mascots. During the Dark Ages the hounds were used as war dogs to haul men off horseback and out of chariots, and there are many tales in Irish mythology of their bravery in battle. There have been twelve more since, all named after Irish high kings or heroes. Originally, the mascot was in the care of a drummer boy, but is now looked after by one of the regiment's drummers and his family. The Irish Guards are the only Guards regiment permitted to have their mascot lead them on parade.

The other type of mascot, usually a dog, was the unofficial mutt which many a soldier has adopted in-situ as a companion.

Dogs play a companionship role post-conflict as well, helping servicemen rehabilitate physically and mentally after the horrors of war. In late 2001, President Bush signed a law authorising the Veterans Administration to underwrite programs like Canines for Combat Veterans to assist with the rehabilitation of US servicemen.

Many veterans, after suffering traumatic injuries, are fighting to get their independence back, and dogs give them a sense of that. Service dogs are 24/7 companions that can retrieve and carry objects, open doors, call attention to safety hazards, help with stress and balance difficulties, and provide a bridge back to society. Operation Freedom, a partnership between the Veterans Administration and Freedom Service Dogs, Inc., pairs specially trained service dogs with returning military personnel and disabled veterans to assist with the lifelong transition from active duty and combat to civilian life.

Anecdotal evidence has existed for years that pets provide positive health benefits, such as blood pressure and stress reduction, but more recently, scientific studies have been conducted to determine the validity of pet therapy in combat. Bringing therapy dogs into Iraq will take dogs to the next level on the battlefield. In June 2010 two black labrador retrievers, Budge and Boe, were deployed to Iraq to help relieve combat stress of soldiers in the field. They provide emotional comfort through physical interactions such as playing fetch or simple petting.

SEARCH AND RESCUE

Search and rescue (SAR) operations by the military are not new. During World War I the first full-time, devoted use of dogs to SAR operations was established. These came in the form of Red Cross dog teams and teams from similar international organisations, who initially trained dogs to go into no-man's land and attend to wounded soldiers.

The dog could simply find an injured soldier and return to his master indicating to him that he had located an individual and would return once more to the spot this time with his master. Some dogs would stay with the injured soldier and bark until help arrived. Some would remain in situ, having medical supplies attached to a harness that the injured soldier could use to attend himself. The one thing evident in all cases is the immense physiological and moral boost the injured soldier has knowing he is not alone.

Some SAR dogs operated in groups, such as sled dogs in World War II who rescue downed pilots in Alaska who were transporting Lead Lease plans. Similar dog units rescued Allied servicemen in Greenland. Today, sled dog teams of the Danish military still patrol this area using the same methods.

Today, it is mostly civilian canine groups who perform SAR operations, rather than the military. Recently, more than 50 international SAR teams consisting of more than 1700 people and about 175 dogs responded to the Haiti earthquake. These heroes are responsible for saving the lives of more than 130 people, while an estimated 200,000 souls were killed. Most of these teams were provided by civilian organisations from around the world.

Canines help search teams to locate victims using their incredible sense of smell to detect live human scent, even from a victim buried deep in rubble. Although the exact processes are still debated they may include skin rafts (scent-carrying skin cells that drop off living humans at a rate of about 40,000 cells per minute), evaporated perspiration, respiratory gases, or decomposition gases released by bacterial action on human skin or tissues. All of this is affected by time and environmental conditions. No wonder we cannot rely on a machine to do the job.

UNITED KINGDOM

The Royal Army Veterinary Corps (RAVC) is one of the smallest corps in the British army, yet it provides invaluable support to the army's animals and serves worldwide with them today. In the years leading up to World War I, most countries had been concentrating on building up their war dog establishments. One notable exception was the British army. At the start of the war Britain had a single guard dog in the Second Battalion of the Norfolk Regiment. This dog was killed in action at Aisne. The British were in no way unfamiliar with the use of war dogs. Throughout time, British warriors, both indigenous to the British Isles or various invading armies, have used war dogs in battles.

Britain can thank the drive and energy of Lt Col E H Richardson for the establishment and operational deployment of British war dogs in 1916. His war dog school, the last European war dog school to be set up, was established in the coastal area of Essex. As would prove the norm in World War II, Britain put a call out to its population to donate dogs to the war effort. In all thousands of dogs served the colours. Many would never return to the homes they came from.

There was no particular breed used by the British army. Airedales were favoured as guard dogs; greyhound crosses, collies and lurchers were used as messenger dogs. But everything in between, big and small, was used. German shepherds, by far the most commonly used military working dog (MWD) today, were renamed alsatians in World War I due to anti-German sentiment.

In World War I many dogs were trained as sentry guards because they were able to smell or hear the enemy from up to a kilometre away depending on conditions. This duty was particularly in demand in the trenches at night, as the Germans conducted forward reconnaissance and attempted to capture Allied soldiers for intelligence gathering. Alert sentry dogs gave advanced notice of approaching enemy forces. Others had messages placed in their collars which were carried from trench to trench. Messenger dogs came into their own at night or in foggy conditions when carrier pigeons could not operate. This was one of the initial convincing reasons for employing dogs in the first place, as the War Office was appalled by the amount of human dispatch carriers being killed. Alas, many messenger dogs became useless as British troops would feed them. Because the dog's training relied on food reward as a stimulus to return to its handler, the well-meaning acts of the forward troops ruined their effectiveness. Some dogs were taught to lay telephone lines between the trenches. Rolls of wire were attached to their backs and dogs ran or crawled between dead man's land and headquarters. Due to their low silhouette and camouflage (dogs were painted black if showing any white areas) their actions resulted in fewer human casualties.

After battles, as soldiers lay injured, ambulance dogs were sent to carry food and medical supplies into no man's land. They did this by crawling from cover to cover, swimming across water obstacles or negotiating wire entanglements. These dogs not only saved lives by supplying medications and bandages, they also gave comfort to and improved morale among injured troops. It must have been a great relief to soldiers, lying wounded in no man's land believing they were forgotten, to hear the footsteps and panting breath of a first-aid carrying dog. It has been stated that the French used 3,000 ambulance dogs, who are credited with saving up to 100,000 lives.

Light haulage dogs were trained to carry ammunition in World War I. This practice was still being used by the British Expeditionary Force (BEF) in the Eastern Command in World War II.

After World War I it did not take the British peacetime government long to reduce defence spending. One of the first services to go was the dogs. The main argument was that technology would make war dogs obsolete. This same argument is still used today, but in the 21st century, MWDs are on the increase as never in the previous hundred years. In 1942 the British army in World War II set up another war dog school, this time in commandeered greyhound racing kennels in Potters Bar. This time the German shepherd was widely used, proving superior in intelligence, stamina, loyalty and courage.

The only animals included on the British Invasion Force plans of World War II were guard dogs of the Royal Military Police (RMP), a small number of Parachute Regiment patrol dogs and mine detection dogs (MDDs) of the Royal Engineers (RE). MDDs were found to be far superior to metal detectors operated by men. For one thing, a mine detection dog could detect wooden, plastic and glass mines laid by the Germans. They could also detect disturbed earth where mines were laid and cover greater areas in quicker time than human and technology counterparts. This role would prove itself again decades latter in 1982 when the RAVC used MDD teams to locate unexploded mines laid by Argentinean forces after the Falkland Islands War.

The RAVC was founded on 25 June 1796, a date now recognised as John Shipp Day. John Shipp was the first veterinary surgeon commissioned into the army. For over two hundred years since John Shipp first joined, the RAVC has been a positive influence in the development of good practice in the care and use of animals for military purposes.

RAVC personnel have been present at every campaign undertaken by the British army since then. Initially concerned with horses for its first 150 years, in 1946 the RAVC became responsible for managing all the army's dog resources. Between the two world wars a large number of veterinary officers served in India, which had an extensive animal establishment, in particular mules and horses.

In 1939, on the outbreak of World War II, forces saw the need for the RAVC to expand rapidly from 190 to nearly 4,500 personnel before hostilities ended in 1945. While most personnel were to serve with equines during World War II the RAVC developed its interest in the use of dogs for military purposes in order to ensure its post war survival. It was fortunate that the RAVC had developed wartime skills in the training and deployment of dogs, since the post war involvement in equines was to decline rapidly.

In 1942 the RAVC became responsible for the procurement of dogs for all service agencies. RAVC personnel ran the Army Dog Training School, which was first located at the Greyhound Racing Association kennels at Potters Bar near London and, in 1945 as an RAVC unit, moved to Belgium and then to Sennelager in Germany. This unit continues to provide technical support for all animals on the continent and still occupies those same premises today. The RAVC also required a permanent depot and moved to the old Remount Depot at Melton Mowbray in 1946, where it remains to this day as the Defence Animal Centre.

The years since 1946 have been active for the RAVC, with corps representation in some form in nearly every theatre of operation. Dogs are an invaluable aid to ground troops in jungle warfare, as was demonstrated in the Malayan campaign against Communist terrorists and again in Borneo against the Indonesian invasion. In Malaya and Borneo during the 1950s and 1960s, dogs worked as trackers seeking out insurgents. In Hong Kong dogs were trained to detect and apprehend illegal immigrants. In Malaya RAVC dog specialists played a significant role in the training of US military personnel for deployment with dogs in Vietnam. Over open country or in urban areas, in pursuit of intruders or detecting their munitions dumps, dogs have been successfully used in Kenya, Cyprus, Hong Kong, Bosnia, Kosovo, Northern Ireland, Iraq and Afghanistan. Dogs have been more widely used around the world to protect military installations and vital points. Their superior ability to indicate the presence of an intruder, coupled with their agility and speed in chase and apprehension, make dogs a formidable deterrent that is rarely challenged by the ill-intentioned. One handler and dog can cover an area that might otherwise require five separate foot patrols, and they can also do it more effectively. The well-trained dog and handler are a very effective and efficient force multiplier. Little wonder that, with the escalation of international terrorism, there has been little abatement in the corps involvement with service dogs.

The RAVC veterinary technician is responsible for overseeing all aspects of the health and welfare of military animals and support veterinary officers (VOs). VOs are capable of providing professional advice on a wide range of issues, including animal employment, disease control and bio-security.

RAVC technicians and VOs are combatants and do not wear the Red Cross armband.

No history about British military dogs could be complete without commenting on the Army Dog Unit Northern Ireland (ADU NI RAVC) Established from 1973 to 2007 as part of Operation Banner, it is the longest running deployment in British Army history. Key responsibilities included 40 guard dog handlers to cover Magilligan and Maze Prisons.

The ADU NI expanded from a couple of handlers in the early days to closer to a 100 in later years. Unit results include the apprehension of eleven high-risk terrorist prisoners, ten terrorists tracked down immediately after an incident, and over 14 tonnes of arms and explosives located by search dogs. Their protection value was such that no establishment was ever broken into where dogs guarded. In 2007 the unit had its colour parade to signify the end of Operation Banner and the unit became the 104 Military Working Dog Support Unit, the third operational RAVC unit.

The Defence Animal Centre (DAC) is a training centre based in Melton Mowbray, east Leicestershire, that trains animals (mainly dogs) for all three armed forces. As well as British defence organisations, it prepares dogs for the UK Immigration Service, HM Prison Service, HM Revenue and Customs, other UK government agencies and overseas agencies. DAC also provides training for Lebanese Defence Force and the Saudi Homeland Security Service, Royal Air Force (RAF) police dog handlers and Ministry of Defence (MOD) Police. RAF Police dogs began to be trained at the Centre from 1994, after merging RAF and Army dog training in April 1991. The centre trains about 300 dogs a year, taking about four to six months to train. The Services Veterinary Hospital looks after the health of all the dogs (Canine Division) and horses (Equine Division) of the UK armed forces.

Following basic military training, dog handlers commence corps training at the DACin Melton Mowbray, and will initially train up to Class 3 standard, allowing them to handle protection dogs. Once experience and knowledge are gained, progression through to Class 1 teaches training, instructing and kennel management. Currently dog trainers are serving in Cyprus, Germany, Brunei, Iraq, Afghanistan, UK mainland and Northern

Ireland. Recently dog trainers have been dispatched to Botswana, Kenya and Australia.

Even though it is the primary MWD user and training organisation in the British forces, the RAVC does not complete this task alone. Firstly, many of the previous deployments as guard dog handlers have been from regiments serving in operational areas: for example, the Parachute Regiment might supply ten members to be trained as handlers while in situ. Secondly, at DAC the RAVC share many MWD training appointments with the Royal Air Force Police (RAFP). The RAVC has also trained dog teams during their existence for other regiments in the British army such as the Royal Military Police (RMP). The RAVC has also had a tradition of training handlers from other countries in the Malaya conflict, including ANZAC (Australia and New Zealand Army Corps) units.

In 1961 in Singapore all guard dogs from No 5 Dog Company Royal Military Police were taken over by new Ghurkha handlers, becoming 5 Ghurkha Dog Company Military Police. Some of these dogs were even selected as compound dogs, which meant they were locked inside a compound without a handler. An RAVC handler was on standby if their dog caught anyone. This is a practice no longer used. More recently, patrol dogs were the most common RAVC dogs in Bosnia and Herzegovina. They are employed as an essential part of camp security as the dogs are an excellent deterrent to would-be intruders. The more aggressive of these dogs are also used for crowd and riot control.

Camp Bastion's Military Working Dog Support Unit is made up of dogs and handlers from 102 Logistic Brigade, part of the RAVC, as well as from the RAFP. Seventeen handlers look after the dogs in Afghanistan, spread from Kabul to the volatile Green Zone in Helmand province, with Camp Bastion as the base. Trained to sniff out explosive ordnance or stop intruders on a base, the military dogs deployed in Afghanistan can often be the difference between life and death for UK personnel. But the dogs are only one half of a team. Handlers and dogs are used for tasks that include searching vehicles coming into Camp Bastion and other forward operating bases and going out on patrols with the infantry, checking routes in advance of convoys for mines or other explosives.

The dogs and handlers from 102 Logistics Brigade, based at Sennelager in Germany, like the RAF teams based at RAF Waddington, train at their bases before deploying to Afghanistan. The handlers deploy for between four and six months. The dogs, however, stay on, so when new handlers arrive they have to start the process of relationship building again.

Royal Marines

The Malaysia agreement dated 9 July 1963 was between the Federation of Malaya, the United Kingdom, North Borneo, Sarawak and Singapore. It was agreed that the states of Sabah, Sarawak and Singapore would be joined with the Federation of Malaya, comprising the states of Pahang, Trengganu, Kedah, Jahore, Negri Sembilan, Kelantan, Selangor, Perak, Perlis, Penang and Malacca, and that the Federation should thereafter be called Malaysia. The perceived fear related to the formation of Malaysia had been exacerbated by the Communists who set up the anti-government party known as the Clandestine Communist Organisation (CCO). The Royal Marines (RM) was therefore faced with a threat on the border from Indonesian-based terrorists, and possibly internally by an armed uprising by the CCO.

With the creation of Malaysia, political and military antagonism between Malaysia and Indonesia developed and led to what was known as the Indonesian Confrontation. Dogs played an important role and the first approved course for training RM dog handlers was completed at the end of June 1963. German shepherds used by the unit on operational activities came mainly from the United Kingdom and Germany. They arrived quite inexperienced and were then trained by the No 2 War Dog Training Unit under the supervision of the RAVC, which then had units in Cyprus, Kenya, Hong Kong and Germany. In recent times the Royal Marines have been teamed with MWD from the RAVC to guard their facilities in the Balkans.

Military Provost Guard Service

In the United Kingdom, changes to the structure of the army due to the increased threat of terrorist attack have resulted in the creation of the Military

Members of the RAAF military working dog section conduct patrols inside and outside the wire to protect RAAF assets. RAAF MWD handlers work with Air Defence Guards, Army MWD teams and Special Forces.

Sapper Shaun Ward and his explosive detection dog (EDD) take up a position ready for helicopter transport prior to a search for Taliban weapons caches. The EDD dogs are very effective.

Poland has military dog handlers in Afghanistan and Iraq. An MWD team above searches a truck at a vehicle checkpoint for Narcotics. All MWDs have an increased role to play on the home front as well as fighting on distant shores.

MWDs await helicopter training, note their protective goggles.

The Finnish army regularly trains in tactical operations working alongside groups of friendly forces under fire, which is vital to enable dogs become familiarised with their surroundings and the sounds of gunfire prior to operational deployments.

Training multiple MWDs side by side to conduct riot control is a difficult task. Members of the army of the Czech Republic are deployed as part of KFOR.

In today's conflicts operations take place in desert conditions. However, recent operations under NATO mandates in locations such as Kosovo have shown that future operations may require MWD teams to operate in Arctic conditions.

Brazilian Military Police about to conduct a hostage rescue situation. MPs use MWDs in both peacetime and war in law enforcement and combat roles.

Russian MWDs were used in Afghanistan in several roles.

In 2010, Sapper Darrin Smith and his explosive detection dog Herbie were killed at a roadside bomb incident in Afghanistan. Sadly they are not the first, nor the last, heroes to give the ultimate sacrifice in war.

Special forces train regularly in escape and evasion avoidance techniques, as they are especially vulnerable to MWDs tracking them down.

For nearly 14 months, Sarbi an Australian Special Forces Explosive Detection dog, was separated from her handler in Afghanistan.

The US War Dog Memorial, located on the grounds of the New Jersey Vietnam Veterans Memorial, Holmdel, NJ. Many similar memorials are finally recognising the war dog's contribution to conflict.

A US Marine Corps dog handler and his military working dog, Marcy, both attached to the US army's 1st Battalion, 18th Infantry Regiment, Task Force 1-77, 1st Armored Division, provide security during a patrol along the Euphrates River in Ramadi, Iraq. The US Marines have a long and proud tradition with MWDs. US Marine Corps photo by Sgt. Edward Reagan.

The Canadian Military MWD program is on the increase again since Canadian Commanders have seen their value on operations in Afghanistan.

US Army Sgt. Kyle Harris stands watch with dog Max, a military working dog, during a joint search and patrol conducted by US soldiers and the Iraqi National Police on 29 November 2008, in the Hadar community of Baghdad, Iraq. US Navy photo by Petty Officer 2nd Class Todd Frantom.

A German 'Fallschirmjäger' dog handler quickly pulls his working dog off an assistant during a canine demonstration by the German army at Mubarak Military City in Egypt.

Provost Guard Service (MPGS). This is a relatively newly formed area of service and lies within the Provost Branch of the Adjutant General's Corps under the direction of Provost Marshal (Army). The aim of the MPGS is to rationalise guarding arrangements at sites where soldiers normally live and work. The MPGS replaces previously civilian-held duties with highly trained, experienced and armed soldiers. MPGS dog handlers are paid an extra allowance. To become a dog handler, a member must first serve in the MPGS as a guard for two years. The exception to this is if the member has previously served as an MWD handler within the military.

Royal Air Force

The work undertaken by RAF Police dogs in theatre is invaluable, and they are considered a key asset for the commander. Providing specialist arms explosive search capability and force protection, they act as a force multiplier, allowing a commander greater flexibility with their personnel while delivering maximum effect on the ground. In some situations the MWD team can do the same amount of work as ten personnel.

RAF Police dogs provide an essential force protection component to military operations worldwide. Since 1945 RAF Police dogs have been employed in the protection of RAF airfields and military assets, the recovery of evidence, the maintenance of public order, the detection of drugs and in anti-terrorist operations. On an operational front, RAF Police dogs have served or are currently serving in Ghan, Misera, Singapore, Aden, Hong Kong, Northern Ireland, Falkland Islands, Bosnia, Kosovo, Diego Garcia, Gibraltar, Cyprus, Kuwait, Saudi Arabia, Iraq and Afghanistan.

The RAF has a long and distinguished history with dogs. It has become world famous for its entertaining dog demonstrations during military tattoos. Sadly, due to budget cuts, these displays have been assigned to history.

Most people who may have come into contact with a RAF Police dog have done so while it was patrolling UK military airfields. Signs warning that dogs are on patrol can be seen on perimeter fences.

There is of course much more to the RAF Police dog section than the image of an aggressive guard dog protecting Britain's frontline fighter squadrons, even though the defence against sabotage has always been a vital part of their work. As in all deterrent claims, which by virtue of their success cannot be given a true figure, the RAF Police dogs must have saved the UK defence budget hundreds of millions of pounds over the years.

MWDs enter RAF service between the ages of eighteen months and three years. Providing they are fit and healthy, dogs can serve until they are approximately nine or ten years old. During their working career the dogs are employed in specialisations, depending on the breed of dog. All RAF dog handlers go through basic police training before proceeding to an MWD course. RAF dog handlers can specialise in several areas including firearms and explosives, and vehicle or drug search roles, as well as carrying out patrol duties in the United Kingdom and overseas.

RAF History

Lt Col J Y Baldwin had served in the trenches in France during World War I, and was impressed by the way the Germans used their war dogs to good effect, not only in the guarding role but also to locate their wounded men and to pull their ammunition supplies around the battlefield. The dogs, many of which were German shepherds, possessed a keen nose, speed, endurance, aggressiveness and above all, courage. In addition, they seemed able to adapt to all types of weather conditions.

Baldwin was so impressed by what he had seen that he later discussed the matter with a close friend, Captain Moore Brabazon, who was at the time serving with the Royal Flying Corps. After the war ended, Baldwin left the army, established his own breeding kennels and became something of an expert on the subject of the alsatian. Baldwin maintained his close links with Moore Brabazon, who, after leaving the Royal Flying Corps, went into politics. When war broke out again in 1939, Brabazon was appointed as the Minister of Aircraft Production responsible for thousands of expensive aircraft and a large number of airfields and storage depots around the country. With the increasing threat of espionage and sabotage, he was deeply troubled with the problem of providing adequate security cover for his assets. Remembering the conversation he had shared with Jimmy Baldwin some years earlier on the subject of dogs, he turned to him for advice and assistance and, in the end, Baldwin was able to persuade him that dogs were the most effective and economical method of guarding his interests. Convinced that dogs were the only economical way ahead, Brabazon obtained the necessary authority from the government to form the Ministry of Aircraft Production Guard Dog School and, as a consequence, Baldwin was offered and accepted the appointment of dog adviser and chief training officer. However, the actual administration of the school was to be carried out by the RAF. In November 1942, Flight Lieutenant Hugh Bathurst-Brown was ordered to command the newly formed Ministry of Aircraft Production Guard Dog School.

Bathurst-Brown, having received his posting notice from the Air Ministry, reported to Woodfold, the site of the new school ten kilometres (six miles) from Gloucester. While Woodfold turned out to be a comfortable, requisitioned country manor house, set in its own pleasant grounds, the facilities made available to the school turned out to be rather sparse and consisted of a garage, which was used as the school's headquarters and administrative centre, and several stables around a courtyard which were used to kennel the dogs. An RAF sergeant was posted to assist Bathurst-Brown in setting everything up, but it turned out to be several more weeks before any further staff or, indeed, any dogs arrived to join them.

Baldwin had handpicked his staff very carefully and they consisted of some of the top dog trainers and breeders from around the country. The dogs that were trained at the school were all donated by the public and consisted of a wide variety of breeds. As soon as the training program got underway, student dog handlers arrived from both the RAF and the United States 9th American Air Force to undertake their initial six-week training course.

At the end of the war, it seemed there was a real possibility of disbanding the Ministry of Aircraft Guard Dog Training School, so Squadron Leader Barnes arranged for the Provost Marshal to meet Colonel Baldwin and view a demonstration of what the dogs and their handlers could do. The Provost Marshal was extremely impressed with what he saw and when he returned to London he suggested that the Ministry of Aircraft Guard Dog Training School should be taken over by the RAF Police and that dogs would be a very cost effective and efficient way of protecting airfields and their valuable assets. During the German V1 rocket campaign, RAF Police dogs helped emergency services in locating buried victims, and in four months managed to find more than 500 trapped people. With severe rationing and the increased pace of wartime life it was impossible for many people to retain pets, and a public appeal for dogs to help guard defence assets had been well received. However, when war ended, owners wanted their pets back. Each discharged dog received a medical check-up and its owner was presented with a certificate declaring that their dog had done its bit for king and country in time of war.

Making the dog school part of the RAF Police organisation was a successful venture. At Woodfold on 24 March 1944, the first batch of RAF Police NCOs commenced their training as dog handlers. In 1946, the newly retitled RAF Police Dog Training School moved from its cramped accommodation at Woodfold to a larger premises at RAF Staverton. Although Baldwin remained as the chief training officer, the school was commanded for the first time by an RAF provost officer, Flight Lieutenant R D Cooper.

In early June 1947, the Three Counties Agricultural Show was held on the Staverton airfield and was attended by a huge audience. One of the biggest and most popular attractions of the day turned out to be the parade of some forty smartly turned out RAF Police dog handlers and their dogs, led by Flight Lieutenant Cooper. By 1948 the training of all RAF Police dogs and their handlers was firmly under the control of the branch, with Colonel Baldwin still in charge of all operational training.

The overall situation took a turn for the best when in June, at the Olympia Stadium in London, the newly formed RAF Police Dog Demonstration Team, using their German shepherds, appeared for the very first time at the Royal Tournament. Sadly, after forty-five years during which millions of people had been thrilled and excited by their spectacular and professional public performances, the RAF Police Dog Demonstration Team disbanded on 18 September 1994. Thankfully they were seen once again in 2009.

In 1949, in response to a request from the Commissioner of Police from the Federation of Malaya for RAF Police assistance, two RAF Police dog handlers, Corporals Stapleton and Thackray, were sent out to the Federation Police Training School in Kuala Lumpur where they successfully organised and assisted in the training of a number of civil police dogs. The dogs were subsequently used in numerous police operations against bandits in the difficult jungle territories.

During February 1951, the RAF Police Dog Training School moved from RAF Staverton to RAF Netheravon, on the edge of the Salisbury Plain.

Eleven RAF Police dogs and their handlers, under the command of Flight Lieutenant G Innes, appeared in Hong Kong in April 1953 on a public parade for the first time in the colony to celebrate the birthday of Her Majesty the Queen.

Lt Col Baldwin retired in October 1953, after thirteen years as the inspiration for the RAF Police Dog Training School, which had, over that period, gone from strength to strength, earning a high reputation in very wide circles.

On 16 June 1954, the first four members of the United States Air Force Police arrived at the RAF Police Depot at RAF Netheravon, where they began a program with the Dog Training School. Although personnel from the US Army Air Force had been trained as dog handlers by the RAF during World War II, they were the first policemen to become qualified dog handlers with the USAF.

During August and September 1960, the RAF Police School moved home once again to RAF Debden, which was situated five kilometres (three miles) southeast of Saffron Walden in the county of Essex.

In 1963, with brand new facilities, the RAF Police Dog Training School joined the depot at RAF Debden and RAF Netheravon closed soon after. In 1975 the RAF Police School moved from RAF Debden to RAF Newton.

By 1982 the RAF Police had been working with dogs for some forty years and had earned for themselves a reputation second to none. Not only were patrol dogs being trained, but the specialist training of dogs to detect the presence of drugs and explosives had been a very successful venture. In 1984 the RAF Police School was detached to Thailand to assist in the training of a number of their air force dogs to detect firearms and explosives.

On 24 February 1991, the Coalition ground offensive into Kuwait began in the Middle East. After only four days, the territory was liberated and the Iraqi forces swiftly defeated. As the overall operation was completed in a very short space of time, a huge number of Iraqi prisoners of war (POW) were suddenly captured by, or surrendered to, the Coalition forces, making the task of guarding them a momentous commitment. To assist in overcoming the problem, RAF Police dog handlers were instantaneously deployed to the prisoner of war compounds, known as the 'Mary Hill Camp'. The number quickly rose to around 4,000 prisoners. The RAF Police dog teams were used on a variety of tasks, providing twenty-four hour coverage at the camp. Apart from being used to patrol the perimeter wire of the enclosures containing the captured Iraqi troops, dog teams were also used to escort prisoners from the Chinook helicopters that brought them into the camp. The teams worked hard in extremely difficult conditions and it was fairly common for a single dog team to be controlling upwards of four hundred prisoners at a time. By 11 March, all the prisoners had been transferred from the Mary Hill Camp over to the camps set up by the US Army and, accordingly, the RAF Police dog teams were stood down from their guarding task.

NORTH AND CENTRAL AMERICA

USA

Considering the ever-increasing use of military working dogs (MWDs) in the US forces today, it is surprising that the USA was one of the slowest countries to initially adopt them.

As Europeans expanded into the New World, so did their dogs. Perhaps the first war dogs in America were those used especially by the Spaniards against Indigenous Americans, who in turn used dogs for their own purposes, such as camp guards or early warning systems. Many of the United States' founders saw the effectiveness of dogs in battle and used them whenever they could.

Benjamin Franklin said in 1775: 'Dogs should be used against the Indians. They should be large, strong and fierce; and every dog led in a slip string, to prevent their tiring themselves by running out and in, and discovering the party by barking at squirrels, etc. Only when the party comes near thick woods and suspicious places they should turn out a dog or two to search them. In case of meeting a party of the enemy, the dogs are all then to be turned loose and set on. They will be fresher and finer for having been previously confined and will confound the enemy a good deal and be very serviceable. This was the Spanish method of guarding their marches.'

Later, the employment of war dogs was urged by John Penn, the lieutenant governor of Pennsylvania, between 1763 and 1771. In a letter to James Young, Paymaster and Commissioner of Muster he proposed that: 'every Soldier be allowed three shillings per month, who brings with him a strong dog that shall be judged proper to be employed in discovering and pursuing the savages.'

But no action was taken, not even after the Revolutionary War of 1776. In 1779, yet another plea for war dogs was made, this time by William McClay of Pennsylvania's Supreme Executive Council.

'I have sustained some ridicule for a scheme, which I have long recommended, that of hunting the scalping parties with horsemen and dogs,' he wrote in 1779, recalling that 'it was in this manner, that the Indians were extirpated out of whole countries in South America.'

Interestingly, at the height of modern warfare, a new generation of leaders stated: 'The capability they [MWDs] bring to the fight cannot be replicated by man or machine. By all measures of performance their yield outperforms any asset we have in our inventory. Our Army (and Military) would be remiss if we failed to invest in this incredibly valuable resource.' (General David H Petraeus, US Army 2008.)

The first recorded use of dogs by the United States army was during the Second Seminole War, and not, as previously thought, the Spanish-American War. Thirty-three Cuban-bred bloodhounds were bought at a cost of several thousand dollars and five handlers were used by the US army to track the Seminole Indians and the runaway slaves they were harbouring in the swamps of western Florida and Louisiana.

During the Spanish-American War in 1898, dogs were used as scouts for Teddy Roosevelt's Rough Riders' horseback patrols in the dense jungles of Cuba. Each of these 'war dogs' were trained as point scouts. Ambushes by the enemy became near impossible; the lessons learned in Cuba by the US Corps were later proven again in the many Pacific Island jungle conflicts against Japan during World War II and again much later in Vietnam by US troops.

In 1885 the German Army Dog School wrote and published the very first training manuals for war dogs, which were later translated by a US army officer and published in the *United States Service Journal* in 1904. However, at the beginning of World War I, America did not have a war dog policy, even though other countries, such as Germany, France and Belgium proved their value. In the spring of 1918 the General Headquarters of the US Expeditionary Force recommended that dogs be used as sentries and messengers, and for patrol and special supply missions. It was proposed to procure enough dogs from French training centres every three months to equip each US division with 228 each. However, the project was not approved by G-3, General Headquarters, and the idea was dropped.

World War II

The army still had no plans for training dogs when the United States entered World War II. The attack upon Pearl Harbor and the sudden entry of the United States into the war greatly stimulated interest in the use of dogs for sentry duty. At the time of Pearl Harbor sled dogs were the only working dogs employed in the army. About fifty of these animals were assigned to military stations in Alaska, where they were used when snow and ice precluded other transport. In 1941 dogs were used by the Air Corps Ferrying Command to rescue airmen forced down in snowbound and desolate parts of Newfoundland, Greenland and Iceland. As World War II started in Europe, and the US army began to prepare for its coming role, it was estimated that 200 dogs might be needed. In actuality, about 10,000 dogs had been trained for the army, navy, Marine Corps and Coast Guard by the time the war ended in 1945.

The first effort to procure and train dogs for the US military was based on volunteers. A civilian organisation, Dogs for Defense, Inc. was formed in January 1942 to work with qualified civilian trainers, who offered their services without pay. In the summer of 1942 a new training program was developed, and responsibility for procuring, handling and training dogs was placed with the Quartermaster Remount Branch.

With the rapid expansion of industrial plants and army installations during the war the threat of potential damage that might be done by saboteurs or enemy agents saw an increase in the use of army guard dogs. By early 1942 German submarines began to operate in large numbers near the Atlantic and Gulf coasts and the landing of saboteurs was a possibility. It was at this time the Coast Guard began beach patrols to prevent such landings. In all, the Coast Guard fielded 2,000 dogs. So successful were they that in 1944 the Coast Guard dog trainers were sent to China to train similar beach patrol units there.

In May 1942 the army established the K-9 Corps. Throughout World War II 595 dogs were trained for scouting duties. The war dog platoon, although trained by the Quartermaster Corps (QMC), was a combat unit, not supply. Each squad contained eight dog handlers who trained and handled four scout and four messenger dogs. After training at a Quartermaster War Dog Reception and Training Center, a war dog platoon was attached to an army corps or division as determined by the theatre commander. Its scout and messenger man-dog team were attached to lower units as needed for work with reconnaissance, combat and security patrols, and as needed for communication purposes. The commanding officer of the war dog unit advised the commanders of using units on the proper use of the handlers and dogs. Fifteen war dog platoons served overseas in World War II. Seven saw service in Europe and eight in the Pacific.

Army war dogs were used not only in the Pacific but also in the Europe, China, Burma and India theatres. Some examples are the 38th War Dog Platoon who was attached to the 85th Division in Villa Di Sassonero, Italy and conducted many operations under mountainous conditions. The QM 42nd War Dog Platoon was heavily engaged during the Battle of the Bulge and later transferred to guard supply dumps in Belgium due to the presence of saboteurs. Army war dog platoons were active throughout the Pacific; in New Guinea they were used as patrol and scout dogs in dense jungle. Such dogs were so feared by the Japanese they became a prime target for Japanese snipers. Army war dogs of Company G 106th Regiment 27th Division on Okinawa were often used on patrols at night.

Dogs were used to guard lines of communication support and supply bases as well as operating ahead of line infantry patrols. One regimental commander noted that after using dogs some patrols did not want to go out without them. One study found that whenever war dogs worked the front line, their efforts cut casualties by more than 65 per cent. Similar comments about the effectiveness of dogs were made a few years later in

Korea, again in Vietnam and, today, forward commanders in Iraq echo the same statements.

The QMC retained the mission of dog procurement from that time until the Korean War. Very little was accomplished relative to dog training except in Europe where, since the early days of occupation, many dogs had been used for guarding supply points and aircraft, and for other types of security. Responsibility for training in Europe was by direction of the US commanding general. European forces continued under the jurisdiction of the QMC at their Dog Training School located at Darmstadt, West Germany. Here, Military Policemen from both the army and air force occupation units were trained for sentry dog duty.

On 7 December, 1951, the responsibility of dog training in the United States was again transferred, this time to the Military Police Corps. Early in 1952 the dog training centre, along with the 26th Scout Dog Platoon, was moved from Fort Riley, Kansas to Camp Carson, Colorado, later designated as Fort Carson. Fort Carson could train approximately 86 sentry dog handlers and 380 dogs during any training cycle, now set at eight weeks. Major emphasis was now placed on training sentry dogs, which were considered a more valuable commodity for every branch of the armed services.

Korean War

At the start of the Korean War, the United States Air Force quickly established 12 air bases throughout the Korean Peninsula with major bases located at Kimp'o, Suwon, Osan and Kunsan. Each of the bases was assigned Air Police squadrons, with sentry dog sections of six to eight dogs attached for air base security. The Korean War provided the air force with a testing ground for individual training, unit training and planning. Korea began to define a combat role for the USAF Air Police. By the time the Korean War ended, more than 500 dogs had been used by the combined United Nations ground forces. The US Army was in Korea on occupation duty after World War II and remained in the south after a Communist government was established in North Korea. In 1950, at the outbreak of the Korean War on 25 June, more than 100 army dogs were stationed in Seoul on sentry duty to reduce theft around warehouses and storage areas. Some of these dogs were recruited for combat duty.

When the Korean War began, the 26th Infantry Scout Dog Platoon was in training at Fort Riley, Kansas. They were immediately sent to Korea for combat patrols. On 11 July 1951, the War Dog Receiving and Holding Station was activated at Cameron Station, Alexandria, Virginia, where newly purchased dogs were processed and conditioned before they were shipped to the Army Dog Training Center, Fort Carson. In Korea, the 26th Infantry Scout Dog Platoon quickly established the value of the dogs on patrol and commanders demanded more dogs than the 26th could provide.

On 27 February, 1952, the 26th Infantry Scout Dog Platoon received a citation for its service, reading in part: 'The 26th Infantry Scout Dog Platoon, during its service in Korea, has participated in hundreds of combat patrol actions by supporting the patrols with the services of an expert scout dog handler and his highly trained scout dog. The members of the 26th Infantry Scout Dog Platoon, while participating in these patrols, were invariably located at the most vulnerable points in the patrol formation in order that the special aptitudes of the trained dog could be most advantageously used to give warning of the presence of the enemy. The unbroken record of faithful and gallant performance of these missions by the individual handlers and their dogs in support of patrols has saved countless casualties through giving early warning to the friendly patrol of threats to its security.'

The outstanding results from the 26th Infantry Scout Dog Platoon led to plans for scout dog platoons for each division in Korea, but only five platoons were trained and shipped before the war ended. The 26th Scout Dog Platoon served with honour and distinction in Korea from 12 June 1951 to 26 June 1953. Platoon members were awarded a total of three Silver Stars, six Bronze Stars for valour, and thirty-five Bronze Stars for meritorious service.

The War Dog Receiving and Holding Station at Cameron Station was placed in a stand-by status on 4 May 1954, after peace negotiations had ended the fighting. At the end of the war, scout dogs not assigned to infantry divisions were retrained for sentry work to patrol the demilitarised zone (DMZ) that was established between North and South Korea.

The Army Dog Training Center at Fort Carson was used during the period 1954 to 1957 to train MWDs, largely for the US Air Force. In 1957 the Army centre was deactivated and the responsibility for training was transferred to the Air Force, which established a permanent training center at Lackland Air Force Base, Texas. By the mid-1970s, most army sentry dogs were used in Korea to guard Hawk missile batteries. By 1980 the last army sentry dogs in Korea were turned over to the Korean military or transferred to the Pacific Air Forces (PACAF) dog school for retraining or to be euthanised.

Vietnam

Dogs in Vietnam were used for many purposes. Their keen senses were used to find dangers like ambushes, booby traps and tripwires before they claimed lives. Dogs were also used to set up ambushes, find downed pilots and runaway ambushers, caches of weapons, food and ammunition, and to guard the perimeter of military bases.

The Vietnam war dogs performed four main tasks. Scout dogs walked point in front of unit patrols. This was the most dangerous job for both dog and handler because they were the initial target. These dogs alerted their handlers to ambushes and booby traps. They were well trained, obedient and alert. Sentry dogs defended the perimeter of military bases and were trained to kill.

Tracker dogs were docile canines that pursued fleeing ambushers and located lost soldiers and downed pilots. Water dogs were trained to defend naval bases by sniffing out human scent underwater, where the Viet Cong often used reeds or pieces of hose to breathe. Interestingly even today Norway trains these same types of dogs to detect waterborne saboteurs.

The patrol dogs could sniff out ambushes approximately one kilometre (1,000 yards) away on a good day before shots were fired and lives were lost. They could detect human scent on landmines, booby traps and tunnels. The dogs could hear high-pitched sounds, like the sound of the wind blowing over tripwires. To indicate that they found something, the dogs would give an 'alert.' This was a silent warning that told the handler the dog had located something. The alert could be almost anything. Some dogs' hair stood on end, others crossed their ears, and some stood on their hind legs. The handler had to observe the dog's behaviour very closely so not to miss the alert. When an alert was given, the area was checked out to see what the dog had found.

In Vietnam there were 'small, highly-trained units, usually consisting of five men and a labrador retriever. This group was called a Combat Tracker Team (CTT). They were a composite group and cross-trained, enabling all members to complete the mission. The purpose of CTT was to reestablish contact with the "elusive enemy", undertake reconnaissance of an area for possible enemy activities and locate lost or missing friendly personnel. The methods used in completing the missions were visual and canine tactical tracking. The unit was usually supported by a platoon or larger force and worked well ahead of them to maintain noise discipline and the element of surprise.' (Frank Merrit, President of the US Tracker Dog Association.)

The Vietnam War saw a big increase in the use of dogs in direct combat roles. Jungle patrols were very limited in what the soldiers could see and hear, even more so at night. Their dogs were invaluable in extending the senses. During the Vietnam War the US Army Infantry Centre, Headquarters Detachment Scout Dog (at Fort Benning, Georgia) supervised handlers and dogs for the scout dog training program with two attached platoons, the 26th Infantry Platoon (Scout Dog) and the 51st Infantry Platoon (Scout Dog) (IPSD). The 51st IPSD was later split to equip and man the newly activated 58th Infantry Platoon (Scout Dog). The 58th deployed to Vietnam in February 1968. After training and development at Fort Gordon Georgia, the 60th Infantry Platoon became the first mine and tunnel detector dog platoon and was deployed to Vietnam at Cu Chi on 22 April 1969 in support of the 25th Infantry Division and the 23rd Infantry Division.

Scout dogs were trained for jungle combat in a twelve-week course that started with obedience and advanced to voice and body signals. They were trained to alert differently for the scent of a living person or an inanimate but unfamiliar object. There was specialised training for daytime or night scouting, detecting tunnels, mines, trip wires and booby traps, and guard duty. Some dogs were specialists in one skill while others were cross-trained to perform multiple tasks. Dogs were used for detecting enemy infiltrations into airfields and base camps, alerting on snipers and ambushes, sniffing out hidden enemy base camps, locating enemy underground tunnel complexes, and finding hidden caches of enemy weapons, food and medical supplies.

In October 1966 the army began initial training to provide 14 provisional canine teams to be attached to the most active elements of the infantry, airborne and cavalry divisions and brigades that were in combat. The deployment of the teams was in groups of four teams (a platoon) to an Infantry division and groups of two teams (a detachment) to a brigade. The teams were comprised of five men and one dog. Based on the experiences of the British, black or yellow labrador retrievers were favoured as tracker dogs, in contrast to the German shepherd that filled the ranks of the scout dog platoons.

By far the biggest difference between tracker and scouting dogs is that scouting is a probing activity and used to define an area as to enemy presence without pursuing the enemy, while combat tracking is a highly aggressive action. What is easily forgotten about tracking is that it is a force to be called in for specialised situations: when there has been an attempted ambush or an ambush by the enemy, or when there is suspected enemy activity or verification is needed. In all, eleven US tracker teams and two Australian combat tracker teams supported US troops in Vietnam.

In 1966-67 Police Field Force K-9 teams accompanied joint US and Vietnamese units conducting cordon and search operations in Military Region IV. The team was composed of six Police Field Force members and a security element of men from the 199th Light Infantry Brigade. After the military unit had cordoned off the area the police entered the hamlet with their dogs, checking the identification cards of all inhabitants as well as making a complete search of the area for tunnels, personnel, weapons and supplies. A representative of the Combined Intelligence Staff accompanied the unit on these operations and provided photographs of Viet Cong as well as the blacklists for the district concerned. Offenders were arrested, and the remainder were released.

The build up of US forces in Vietnam created large dog sections at US Air Force Southeast Asia (SEA) bases. Eventually, 467 dogs were assigned to Bien Hoa, Bien Thuy, Cam Ranh Bay, Da Nang, Nha Trang, Tuy Hoa, Phu Cat, Phan Rang, Tan Son Nhut and Pleiku air bases. Within a year of deployment, attacks on several bases had been thwarted when the enemy forces were detected by dog teams. Captured Viet Cong told of the fear and respect that they had for the dogs. The success of sentry dogs was determined by the lack of successful penetration of bases in Vietnam and Thailand. Sentry dogs were also used by the army, navy, and Marines to protect the perimeter of large bases.

Vietnam canine units were credited with saving thousands of lives in the war. There are countless stories of how the dogs prevented an ambush, discovered deadly mines or booby traps, or sounded the alarm against infiltrators. These dogs were so effective that the Viet Cong offered bounties for killing military working dogs and their handlers. Viet Cong troops would be rewarded for bringing a dog's tattooed ear or a handler's patch back.

Between 1964 and 1975 there was a confirmed list of 3,747 dogs identified by ear tattoo who had served in Vietnam as scout and sentry dogs, largely German shepherds. However, it is believed that a total of 4,900 dogs in fact served. The discrepancy is caused by the lack of records before 1968.

Some 10,000 handlers served in Vietnam. Sadly, at the end of the conflict, in a decision that remains painful decades later, most of the in-country dogs were euthanised. Fewer than 204 dogs were returned to the United States or other locations. Handlers were faced with the agonising decision of either euthanising their dog or giving it to the South Vietnamese Army. Black dogs were regarded as bad luck in Vietnam so many labradors had few prospects.

Many handlers today have no idea what ultimately happened to their mates. Did they get a decent burial; did someone say words over their grave; did any suffer when they were left behind? To many veterans these are still America's MIAs, the soldiers whose bodies still lie on distance shores. The decision to leave them there was perhaps not America's finest hour.

Cold War

In the post-Vietnam era, MWDs were predominantly used in a police and security role protecting air bases in Europe and the Philippines.

The use of sentry dogs was limited in the States to Strategic Air Command (SAC) bases with nuclear weapons or other high-priority weapons systems. These dogs were well suited for guarding these areas. The majority of the bases were located in parts of the US not known for having a warm climate.

The patrol dog concept, developed by the Washington DC Police Department, proved that controllable but still aggressive dogs could be effectively used at any military base. The fact that the use of dogs was now considered minimum force instead of extreme force caused a rapid growth of military dog use.

In the 1970s the US Air Force used more than 1600 dogs worldwide. Personnel cutbacks then reduced US Air Force dog teams to approximately 530 stationed throughout the world. However, with recent terrorist attacks this number is again on the increase. By 2004 there were 2,300 MWDs in the Department of Defence (DoD).

The First Gulf War

Iraq invaded Kuwait on 2 August 1990. Operation Desert Shield began on 7 August. Iraq officially accepted ceasefire terms on 6 April 1991. During that time frame there were 118 MWD teams that deployed to the Gulf region for Operation Desert Shield and Desert Storm.

The US employed approximately 118 MWDs during the first Gulf War. Many were used as part of base security by Military Police detachments. Several coalition forces deployed dogs, the largest being France at more than one thousand. The physical sight of an MWD conducting searches at the entrance of a facility would have deterred would-be terrorist or criminal elements from entering the camps. No bases guarded by US service dogs were compromised during the first Gulf War.

Training Military Handlers and Dogs Today

The 341st Training Squadron, formerly known as the Department of Defence Military Working Dog School is located at Lackland Air Force Base, Texas.

The peacetime mission of the dogs includes drug intervention along the southern borders of the United States in support of Homeland Security. The 341st trains drug detection dogs and handlers for major air, land and sea ports-of-entry to the United States in a joint counter-drug effort with the US Customs Department and other federal drug law enforcement agencies. Some drug-dog training is conducted in situ on the Mexico–US border.

The 341st Training Squadron has four major sections, divided into logistic, dog training, handler training and medical support to the entire DoD.

The dog training section trains and certifies over 185 explosive detector dogs a year. These working dogs are then shipped worldwide to support the global DoD mission. Another 96 dogs are trained for patrol use only.

The Handlers Course trains over 525 students annually from the air force, army, navy, and Marine Corps. Additionally, they train more 300 working dogs for all of the DoD and Federal Aviation Administration (FAA).

The Supervisors Course gives advanced training and management skills to more than 100 air force, army, navy and Marine students a year.

The Logistics Flight is responsible for shipping and managing more than 1,300 DoD MWDs worldwide. On a single day, as many as 108 dogs may be on assignment. Change has also come in legislature for the benefit of the canines. Prior to 2000, older MWDs were required to be euthanised. Thanks to a new law, retired military dogs may now be adopted. The first adoption was of MWD Lex, a working dog whose handler was killed in Iraq.

The FAA Support Branch trains more than 45 explosive detection dogs annually. About eight dog teams are dispatched each day, year round, to assist in the State Department's Dignitary Protection Program.

Defense Military Working Dog Veterinary Services

Similar to the British army's RAVC, the United States armed forces has a specialised corps to look after defence animal assets. The US Army Veterinary Corps is part of the Army Medical Department. Its primary mission is to protect the war fighter and support the National Military Strategy. Part of the Corps' mission is to provide care to military working dogs, ceremonial horses and working animals of many Department of Homeland Security organisations.

US Air Force

During the Vietnam War, the defense of air force bases mirrored the conflict itself: there was no rear echelon once the entire country became a battlefield. Air force bases, relatively unaffected by ground forces in past wars, were no longer considered safe havens. They, too, suffered from costly ground assaults and mortar shelling.

Within easy reach of North Vietnamese troops, air force bases in Vietnam and Thailand were attacked 478 times from 1964 to 1973. 155 Americans were killed and 1,702 wounded, along with 375 allied aircraft destroyed and 1,203 damaged. In fact, more US planes were lost in ground action (101) than in dogfights with MiG jets (62). In Vietnam 26 per cent of all MWD teams were from the US Air Force.

The attack hammered home a hard message. To fight in the air, the Air Force had to be able to fight on the ground. The answer was the employment of sentry dogs, some of which were legendary for their aggressiveness.

As training methodology improved, drug detector and explosives detector dogs were included in the USAF dog inventory. The present-day dog program owes much to these early days. By the early 1970s many bases had small dog sections, including patrol dogs and specialist detection dogs.

Today the US Air Force MWD teams often work miles from any airfield in support of Army operations in Afghanistan.

Today, of course, the US Air Force is the DoD's lead agency in the use and training of war dogs.

US Marines

As early as 1935, the US Marines Corps (USMC) was interested in war dogs. They had experienced the enemies' sentry dogs in Haiti and in the 'Banana Wars' in Central America, where dogs staked around guerrilla camps in the jungle sounded the alarm at the approach of the Marines.

The Marines thought they would have to fight the Japanese in the Pacific. Since the Japanese were well established in the islands and atolls of the central, south and west Pacific, the Marines knew they were going to be fighting in tropical climates where the vegetation provided jungle-like coverage. In such conditions, dogs would be ideal sentries and couriers. It was no surprise later that the Marine Corps had the first large dog unit in the nation's history to see action against the enemy.

Marine messenger dogs were taught to carry messages, ammunition or special medical supplies from one handler to another handler, avoiding all other men. They were subjected to overhead rifle and machine gun fire and explosions of heavy charges of dynamite and TNT to simulate an nearly as possible actual battlefield conditions. The Marine sentry dogs were trained to warn troops of the approach or the nearness of any other humans.

The Marine scout dog was trained to alert the troops of the enemy, but not to bark and tell the enemy where the troops were.

USMC's military working dog program, which trains explosive detection dogs (EDDs) and handlers, was first developed during World War II. The USMC started to train dogs and their handlers to be capable of scouting and patrolling during combat operations where the dogs' keen sense of smell enabled Marines to search a larger area in a shorter amount of time.

Unlike other branches of the military, where service members become dog handlers after several years of enlistment, Marines go from boot camp to Military Police school and straight on to the dog handling school after a selective process. While at MP school, individuals interested in the canine field must be in the top 10 per cent of their class. After writing an essay on why they want to be a handler, they will then go before an oral board to get selected for the canine school. Just like the handlers, the dogs also go through a selection process. Dogs begin training when they are nine months to a year old. Like Marines, they go through a basic boot camp to learn the rudimentary skills of being a military working dog. The training can be as quick as a few weeks to as long as several months depending on the dog, but after boot camp it's up to the handler to improve their skills.

During the winter of 1965 the Marines entered into an inter-service agreement with the army to train scout dogs. The United States 1st Marine Corps Scout Dog Platoon arrived in Vietnam (30 Marine Scout Dog Teams) in early March 1966. They were split up and arrived via two C-130 aircraft, 15 teams in each. This was the first time since World War II that Marine scout dogs were deployed in combat. The Marines kennelled their dogs near Da Nang at Camp Kaiser, named after the first Marine scout dog to be killed in action in Vietnam. Between late 1965 and January 1969 four Marine scout dog platoons were deployed to Vietnam. In 1970, after the army's success, the Marines instituted their own mine/tunnel dog program. Approximately 7 per cent of MWD teams in Vietnam were from the USMC.

Typical of the use of USMC MWDs on US military bases today, the Provost Marshal's Office (PMO) at Quantico, Virginia has a six-dog canine section. Each dog is dual-tasked to provide detection in either narcotics or explosives, while maintaining their capabilities as a patrol dog.

Military working dogs have helped Marines on and off the battlefield for years, but their training continues to adapt to new circumstances. To become more familiar in a combat environment, military working dogs and their handlers headed out to San Mateo for field training recently with Military Police Company Combat Logistics Regiment 17, 1st Marine Logistics Group. The dogs were brought out to the field so they could experience a live-fire movement exercise. By working under such conditions, the Marines train their MWDs to get used to things they will encounter on a daily basis when operating with a Marine squad.

Currently the largest commitments are in Afghanistan, where once again the Devil Dog MWD handlers are in the thick of the fighting.

US Army

The US Army has led the way in operations involving MWDs from the US' first use of dogs in combat, through to operating large numbers during World War II. To some extent the air force has replaced the army as the lead agency as far as training and numbers are concerned; however, the army still maintains a formidable MWD force with some specialist skills such as the Airborne K-9 Unit at Fort Benning.

The US Army is heavily involved in conflicts such as those in Afghanistan and Iraq as well as United Nations commitments. Such is the demand for MWDs that many army units have air force, navy or Marine dog handlers attached to them. A lot of the army MWD handlers are drawn from Military Police (MP) units as the Army operates MP MWD teams extensively in peacetime in security and law enforcement roles. An MP MWD handler can find himself working as a patrol team with the 10th Mountain Division in Kabul or riding in a Stryker armoured vehicle in Iraq.

Navy

The navy first used dogs in World War II to guard facilities. US Navy canine operations, (about 2 per cent of MWDs in Vietnam were from the Navy) in Da Nang started with a class of dog handler trainees at Lackland Air Force Base, San Antonio, Texas. Additional handlers and replacements went through training at Lackland as part of regular training 'flights' comprised mostly of air force personnel. A very few navy handlers received their training in the Philippines.

Upon completion of training the handlers and their dogs were loaded on to two C-130s for the 40-hour flight to Da Nang. The kennels at China Beach were ready and waiting when the teams arrived.

The dog's primary mission was mostly fence line patrol. Secondary missions included jeep patrol, narcotics detection and the demonstration team.

In the early years of the SEAL teams there were both officially qualified SEAL dog handlers and those that were trained 'in house'. There were few schools that met the SEAL's 'special' needs, because very few people knew what their area of expertise was. They took official military school curricula and modified them. As a result, a majority of their dog handlers were trained by police departments, rescue squads or emergency crews. The recipients of this training considered themselves dog handlers, as did their team members, but few were documented as such.

Upon completion of the course at Lackland they were sent to an experimental program at the Naval Research Centre in Panama City, Florida. Their main purpose was the detection of enemy swimmers.

It was hoped that the dogs could be employed to guard fixed emplacements such as bridges, outposts near the water's edge and mooring sites for small boats or even large ships. Many developments came from that program, as it became clear that the dogs could do much more than was ever imagined. For example, dogs could be employed to ride aboard small river craft for the detection of enemy swimmers not only on the surface, but underwater as well. Using a zigzag patrolling pattern downwind, these dogs could reliably detect swimmers up to 1.5 kilometres (one mile) away and nine metres (30 feet) deep.

The US Navy have used MWDs post-Vietnam for sentry duty at shipyards, air stations, ordnance plants and ammunition depots. More recently they have dealt with narcotics. Naval Police MWD handlers operate specialist contraband detection dogs as part of daily military law enforcement practice. The navy also operates EDDs as part of the fight against terrorism. Like their air force, Marine and army counterparts, a naval military dog handler can find themselves on a vehicle checkpoint in downtown Baghdad, many miles from any ship or ocean.

At present the navy on Guam uses two breeds, German shepherds and Belgian malinois. These animals are known for their abilities to patrol, as well as their detective work skills. The navy uses MWDs not only on land-based facilities, but also on board vessels.

Deployments Worldwide

The US MWDs are currently employed all over the world. As well as their work in operational zones such as Kosovo, Afghanistan or Iraq, they also fill the crucial role of guarding bases and facilities against the ever-present threat of terrorism. US MWD teams are seen operating in the snow of Alaska and the tropics of Colombia.

Likewise, the MWD handler is no longer expected to stay in his branch of service. As the war in Afghanistan changes, so does the mission of the

K-9 Unit. At a remote location in the north-eastern mountains of Afghanistan, near the Pakistan border, sits a US Army Forward Operating Base. Attached to the US army infantry unit are four dog teams, two air force and two navy, two EDDs and two NDDs. Their mission is to support the Infantry as they flush out and eliminate the Taliban and other terrorists during what is being called the fiercest fighting Afghanistan has seen since the beginning of the war.

Missions in Bosnia are referred to as Peace Support Missions. During daily operations MWDs have been proven to dramatically increase the effectiveness of the soldier. The dogs are used in activities such as guarding, patrolling, searching, closing off areas, riot control, arrest of suspects, mine and explosive detection and providing general security to United Nations personnel. The use of dogs has a vital physiological effect on friendly forces and against opposition forces.

For nearly a century, an estimated 100,000 dogs have served in the United States military. Early on, dogs were donated by the civilian population in order to fill military needs. Later they were specially bred for the job. Dogs have been used by US forces in World War I, World War II, Korea, Vietnam, Persian Gulf, Bosnia and Kosovo. There are approximately 600-700 canines in the Middle East in such places as Kuwait, Afghanistan, Saudi Arabia and Iraq. A vast number are deployed worldwide to support the war on terror. Many MWD instructors and advisers are also stationed in many parts of the world aiding foreign countries' canine programs.

CANADA

For a reasonably large modern defence force involved in many modern conflicts, Canada Forces (CF) have used MWDs on a very limited scale. Canada did not officially use dogs during World War II; however, some regiments had canine mascots, and some POW camps in Canada used local guards' own dogs in a sentry role.

A dog program started in May 1963 in preparation for a joint nuclear program with the United States in Europe. The first group of 18 handlers was trained by the United States (with some German instructors) at Kreuzburg

Kaserne in Weisbadan, Germany. Kennelling facilities were built at the CF base in Zweibrücken, Germany for eighteen dogs. The first contingent came to the base with no scale of issue for this type of operation, so ingenuity had to be used to get the operation up and running. The second wave of handlers was trained again in Weisbaden and returned to the base in Baden, Germany. They had a much easier time of it though, as the Canadian MWD teams were gradually getting a scale drawn up for rations and equipment identified.

In 1967 Canadian dog handlers went to Lahr, Germany to set up a dog kennelling facility, as they were taking over this base from the French Air Force and closing the Zweibrücken base. In the late summer all dogs and handlers from Zweibrücken were housed and operational in Lahr.

In 1970 Lahr was phased out of nuclear weapons, and some of the dogs and handlers were moved to Baden. The dog program was completely phased out in 1973 when Canada ceased to have operational nuclear weapons in Europe.

The nuclear capability role was in joint custody (Canada and the United States) and NATO had a big say in the operation and management of the MWD program. Canada used German veterinarians, who did routine physicals once a month and urgent medical treatment as required. The US Military was still used as the training facility as well as for medical backup. Any major medical problems were handled by US vets in Weisbaden.

As Canadian MWD handlers rotated through the program to replace those returning to Canada, some worked with the Americans in a training capacity and assisting the resident veterinarian. At Weisbaden there were kennelling facilities for 568 dogs. All buying of dogs for the program for Europe and South East Asia was done from this facility as well as the training of handlers for these venues.

Research into canine effectiveness by Sgt Dave Kimbers led him to submit a proposal in early July 2006 recommending the development of a Military Police Service Dog team for the Maritime Forces Atlantic (MARLANT) area. As the CF had long since abandoned its canine programs there was no established policy or framework with which to begin the program. As a result, Sgt Kimbers was selected to implement the program and was tasked to research, write and establish the legal framework. He attended and successfully completed a police canine handler selection course hosted by the Ontario Provincial Police.

The CF use civilian Canadian mounted police dogs during air force training in the Advanced Survival Evasion Resistance Escape (ASERE) courses that run in eastern Manitoba. The course is conducted by the Canadian Forces School of Survival and Aero Medical Training (CFSSAT) at 17 Wing, Winnipeg. During the course, students learn a variety of skills and procedures they could use to survive and be rescued if their aircraft were ever forced down in hostile territory. This includes an actual 36-hour tracking and dog evasion exercise. The students were briefed on the proper reaction procedures if and when the dog finds them during the exercise.

The Royal Canadian Mounted Police (RCMP) had a role as a para-military organisation, especially in the country's early history. Canadian police forces have used dogs for public safety since the mid-1890s. However, the first programs featured sled dogs whose mission was transport, not tracking or patrol work. The all-purpose police patrol dog programs may be traced from 1930, when an informal but important officer/dog team was on the job in Alberta. This partnership led to the formalisation of the program by the RCMP in 1935. At the time of writing there are 121 working teams across Canada. The RCMP dogs are called on to assist the Canadian military as required.

During recent overseas deployments the CF did not possess an integral EDD capability. It became necessary to request a civilian company to explore the possibility of contracting EDDs for force protection of Canadian troops in Afghanistan. The Kabul office of RONCO Consulting Corporation, an international company with vast experience in MDDs and EDDs, was approached. RONCO provided two EDDs and two handlers to work at Camp Julien. Again, a civilian company has come to the aid of the CF this year, the Canadian Landmine Foundation, which set out to fund the training of six mine detection dogs. The dogs will be trained by the Canadian International Demining Corps, and are expected to be deployed in northern

Afghanistan. Australian MWD handlers have also been attached to CF in Afghanistan to provide teams of patrol dogs during combat missions.

MEXICO

Militaries around the world are restructuring in response to new operational environments that blur distinctions between national security and public safety. More often than not, force restructuring efforts are carried out under severe resource constraints and amid complex legal and human rights issues generated by broadened civil-support missions. South of the United States in Mexico, a new force—composed of police, military and national intelligence components—has formed and expanded since the concept was first proposed in late 1998. This new organisation—the Federal Preventive Police (Policía Federal Preventiva or PFP)—has acquired the mandate, resources and missions to transform the way Mexico deals with its most pressing security concerns.

The MWDs of the Military Police's (MP's) Second Brigade of the Mexican army have teamed up to patrol and fight against organised crime with civilian authorities. Due to the current major drug war in Mexico, many MWD resources are used for internal security missions as opposed to war dog roles. An exception is the search and rescue role, where the Mexican Army has recently supplied several teams to assist in natural disasters within the region.

Training of MWDs starts from four months of age through a process of socialisation, where they establish a bond with their handler. The team is then called 'binomial canine', in which the animal is accustomed to work in any environment. They also start learning basic obedience—an indispensable feature for dogs that are selected to work in this elite group. The predominant breeds are Belgian malinois, German shepherd and Rottweiler.

The 37th Military Camp in San Miguel de los Jagueyes is one of Latin America's largest dog sections. Its facilities include modern operating rooms, X-ray and ultrasound equipment and a breeding centre. After receiving four months' initial training, MWDs go for a further eight months at the Canine

Training Centre of the Army (CACEM) in Santa Lucia, Mexico. After a high level of basic training the dogs specialise in search and location of narcotics, search and location of explosives, or guard and protection duties. Those dogs specialising in the detection of narcotics can search vehicles, houses, boats, aircraft, suitcases, facilities and buildings. The Mexican Army use pseudo-scents in training, which have the characteristic smell of the particular drug—in this case heroin, marijuana and cocaine.

Dogs specialising in the detection of explosives are required to reach a higher standard of ability due the role's greater difficulty and deadly nature. Here, the dog is taught never to touch the device but make only a passive indication. In the case of explosives training, real components are used. Guard and protection dogs carry out their work in the role of patrol, hostage rescue, prisoner escort and riot control. The dogs are trained to bite at strategic points such as limbs, back and chest, so that they do not cause too much damage but do incapacitate the offender.

Search and rescue MWD teams go through different stages, the first of which is sociability. The next stage is basic and advanced obedience, where the dog gets used to various obstacles in tight spaces (simulated natural disasters such as a house destroyed by an earthquake or hurricane). The pseudo-scent of rotting corpse is then introduced to the dogs to search for the dead. These dogs can detect this scent more than 5 metres (5.5 yards) underground. Naturally, dogs are also trained to find living persons.

At the end of the stage of specialisation training, the dogs are sent to different national military cells. Depending on their role, the dogs are ready to fight organised crime or provide assistance to victims of natural disasters. About 3,000 MWDs are working throughout the Republic.

General Carlos Enrique Adam, commander of the Mexican Army Military Police said 'MWDs are indispensable to the armed forces mainly in cases of disasters by rescuing people who are under rubble and in the fight against drug gangs.'

SCANDINAVIA

NORWAY

The Norwegian Armed Forces state that there are many reasons for using military working dogs (MWDs). The most important from a Norwegian military point of view is the dog's ability to detect any substance that produces any kind of odour, given the right training. This includes all kinds of objects, from humans to small amounts of drugs, explosives or any relevant matter that would be undetectable by other means. Furthermore, the dog has many other qualities that make it suitable for service, including flexibility, ability to learn, versatility and of course the deterrent effect of a guard or sentry dog that is trained to attack. These make the MWD a valuable tool for any Norwegian commanding officer.

History
The history of the Norwegian Armed Forces (NAF) starts in Sweden in the period 1943-45. Prior to World War II there were a few attempts to start a canine service in the NAF without success.

The Norwegian police unit (*Rikspolitikompaniet*), which was established and trained in Sweden in order to take control in Norway after World War II, used MWDs in their training for operations. The dogs were trained and used in attack, protection and sentry duty, as well as sled dogs in the winter. In the autumn of 1945 the Swedish army provided Norway with 26 trained MWDs and six puppies as a gift. These dogs were commissioned to a camp at the town Ski in November 1945 as a unit in the Army Medical Service.

The unit was moved several times and in 1948 the supreme command decided to terminate the whole service. In the winter of 1949 the dogs were 'temporarily destroyed', as a former commanding officer of the NAF put it, 'in order to avoid killing the dogs'. After some discussions and recommendations the service was re-established in 1951 and the dogs 'magically came back to life'. In 1955 the unit was moved to the island of Rauøy in the Oslofjord, and was under the command of the Coast Artillery Fortress Oslofjord.

In 1959-60 the unit was on the move again, this time to the small town of Drøbak along the Oslofjord. The school was able to establish a functional camp here and stayed there for 43 years. In 2003 the unit was moved to Hauerseter Camp, approximately 60 kilometres (37 miles) north of Oslo, and since August 2009 the unit has been a part of the Norwegian army.

At present there are two main categories of MWDs in service in the NAF:

Patrol dogs, with three sub-categories:
• Service dog 1 (S1): This type of dog is trained to locate personnel in different ways. Basic skills are obedience, patrol duty and tracking. The dogs can be given additional training in other disciplines, for example, avalanche search. Normally this dog is not trained as an attack dog.
• Service dog 2 (S2): The S2 is specialised as an attack dog and is typically used in guard and sentry duty. This dog is also used by some units as support in close quarter battle. One advantage is that the dog is able to neutralise a suspect without use of excessive force, either inside a building or outside to catch runners trying to escape.
• Service dog 3 (S3): The S3 is a complete patrol dog, and is trained in all the disciplines of S1 and S2. This means it is more flexible in use, but it is also more demanding to maintain the skills of the dog and handler. This is the preferred category of MWD in most units.

Detection dogs
The detection dogs (or sniffer dogs) are trained in the following categories:
• drug detection
• explosives detection
• improvised explosive device (IED) detection
• weapons detection

Once a dog is trained and certified in one category, it will not be trained to detect other substances belonging to a different category. All detection dogs are trained to locate and indicate the relevant object or substance in a quick and efficient way. The indication should be passive, for example, sitting or lying down without touching the source of the odour. Depending on the category and the environment the dog is supposed to work in, the search pattern of the dog will vary.

National Service: Army

All branches of the NAF use MWDs. In the army the dogs are used in Military Police (MP) units, in the border guard along the Russian border, and in the Rapid Response Force, Telemark Battalion.

The MP started using patrol dogs in 1988, partly because of a tragic avalanche accident in which 16 soldiers were killed in 1986. Many changes were made following this accident, and one was the increased focus on readiness and rescue training. MWDs were trained for avalanche search, in addition to the normal patrol dog training, and were on call during the whole winter. This practice is still in use today, and the dogs are also used in other search and rescue missions in support of civilian police. The MP also uses explosives detection dogs, and counter-IED dogs.

The border guard use patrol dogs on their long range recon patrols (LRRPs) along the 196-kilometre (122-mile) -long Russian border, and there have been several cases where the MWDs have contributed to the investigation of illegal border crossings by providing evidence.

Telemark Battalion use patrol dogs, as well as explosives detection dogs and counter-IED dogs in their operations abroad.

Air Force

The air force has traditionally had the largest number of dogs in the NAF, mainly in force protection roles. The dogs have been used in sentry duty as part of the security units on the Air Force bases. In the 1970s and 1980s most of the sentry duty was done by so-called 'warning dogs'.

Several dogs were placed in large cages along the perimeter of the camps or high-value targets, and they would alert the dog handler by barking if any intruder was detected. The dog handler and a quick response unit could then respond to this with either the same dog or a second dog to locate the intruder and arrest him. This method allowed a minimum of personnel to guard a large area with an acceptable level of security. The dog's reputation was also important as a deterrent, as they were known to be dangerous to anyone but the handler.

Presently there are no warning dogs in service, as it was difficult to acquire dogs with the right qualities for this kind of work. This kind of dog was often problematic to handle. This would not be a big problem had it not been for the fact that the dogs changed handlers more than once a year, due to the use of conscripts as handlers.

Another factor is the limited supply of suitable dogs. This has led to a change in practice from the earlier years. The military now usually purchases puppies and hands them over to so-called puppy hosts for approximately ten months. At the age of approximately twelve months the dog is evaluated for use as an MWD, and suitable dogs start on a training program that lasts about twelve months. Those not suitable are given away or sold. No dog is destroyed unless it has mental or physical problems that make it unsuitable for civilian use.

The air force now uses all categories of MWDs, except drug detection dogs.

Navy
The Navy has used dogs since 1998 in the Coastal Ranger Command, a unit which has been developed since the decommissioning of the Coastal Artillery. The unit specialises in missions along the coastline, mainly in maritime intelligence, surveillance, target acquisition and reconnaissance (ISTAR). The use of dogs has been successful, and the unit develops tactics and action patterns that allow the dogs to be used in an effective way.

National Guard
The National Guard (NG) uses patrol dogs in their mission as a local territorial force. Most of these dogs are owned by the dog handler, unlike the

others, which are government property. These dogs are tested and evaluated in the same way and meet the same standards as ordinary MWDs, and several NG MWDs and handlers have also served in operations abroad with great success. There are two drug enforcement groups, respectively in the north and the south, that both use drug detection dogs in their efforts to unveil any abuse of illegal drugs in the military. The dogs are used in several different ways, and they provide important direct or circumstantial evidence of abuse that often lead to a prosecution.

Operations Abroad: Danor/Gaza

The first international operation was United Nations Emergency Force (UNEF) in Gaza in the 1950s, where Norway and Denmark established a battalion called Danor. One of the Norwegian contributions to this was a canine unit with ten German shepherds and dog handlers. The dogs were mostly used on sentry duty with good results.

Norbatt/ Unifil

In the spring of 1978 it was decided to establish a canine platoon as a part of the Norwegian battalion Norbatt in the United Nations Interim Force in Lebanon (UNIFIL). During a few very busy weeks the dogs and handlers were gathered at the NAF and given the necessary training before deploying to Lebanon. In the beginning the conditions were quite difficult, with several 'tics' (troops in contact) that demanded a lot from both dogs and handlers.

Mine-search dogs were trained and deployed during the first years due to the high threat level. After the minefields were identified and marked properly, this capacity was not given any priority.

Norway had an infantry battalion permanently in Lebanon for a total of twenty years, and during this time there was always an operational dog platoon available for the battalion commander. In the last ten years the platoon consisted of at least ten patrol dogs, as well as two narcotics detection dogs (NDDs) and one EDD.

The patrol dogs were mainly used in so-called 'ambush patrols' during the nights in order to detect and capture insurgents on the move through the battalion's area of responsibility. The dogs were also used in daytime patrols as a show of force or as a deterrent. The NDDs were mostly used to check the soldiers going on leave, to avoid any drugs being smuggled out of Lebanon by Norwegian troops. The EDD was used at checkpoints and in raids in order to detect bombs or explosive materials.

Kuwait/Saudi Arabia

After Operation Desert Storm in 1991, Norway deployed a Mobile Army Surgical Hospital (NORMASH) to Saudi Arabia in order to support the operations that followed. This unit had two patrol dogs and handlers for force protection purposes. One of the dogs was transferred directly from Lebanon, the other was shipped from Norway.

Somalia (Unisom)

Norway deployed a unit to Mogadishu in 1992, and a total of four MWDs were part of this unit. The dogs and handlers were used in sentry duty as well as for explosives detection.

Balkan

Three Norwegian patrol dogs and handlers were part of the operation United Nations Protection Force (UNPROFOR, Bosnia and Croatia) in 1992–95, mainly in a close protection role for the Norwegian field hospital, as well as support for escort missions.

In 1995 the Norwegian unit was under NATO command as a part of the Implementation Force (IFOR, then Stabilisation Force (SFOR) 1996–98, Bosnia and Herzegovina), and the canine unit also had an explosives detection capability.

In Kosovo (KFOR, June 1999), the Norwegian contribution also consisted of a mine search capability, due to the threat level. The canine unit was used in many different operations, from riot control to search operations by patrol dogs that were given additional training to detect weapons. The EDDs were routinely used in a force protection role to prevent attacks.

Kyrgyzstan

During Operation Enduring Freedom, 2002–2003, the Royal Norwegian Air Force deployed six F-16 fighter planes and necessary support, and a close protection unit with MWDs to an airfield in Kyrgyzstan.

Afghanistan

In the International Security Assistance Force in Afghanistan there has been a canine unit since the start. The unit has been situated in Kabul HQ, later in Mazar el Sharif and finally in Meymaneh as a part of the Provincial Reconstruction Team (PRT).

In 2007, a unit from the Royal Norwegian Air Force had the command over Kabul International Airport (KAIA). The air force also deployed a specialised counter-IED team consisting of EDDs and handlers along with IED operatives, in order to secure the base and operations security. This team worked almost around the clock for six months and prevented several attempts to place bombs inside the airfield.

The canine unit in the PRT consists of two patrol dogs and handlers, one EDD and handler and one counter-IED dog and handler. The use of the canine units has been quite variable, due to changes in the missions and in the capabilities of the whole PRT. Patrol dogs have been used for force protection, and as a support and close protection for snipers. The explosives detection dogs and counter-IED teams have been used for clearance and search operations.

Development

Despite increasing use of high-tech solutions it seems that the MWD is still regarded as a useful tool in military operations nationally and abroad. This is made clear by the fact that every major Norwegian operation with land forces in the past has had a canine unit of some kind attached, and though there have been discussions about the size and configuration of the units, it has seldom been an option to phase out this practice.

This is most likely caused by the MWD's flexibility, and its ability to adapt to new tasks, conditions and challenges as the missions change. The skills and capabilities of the dog handlers (and those who task them) are of course also an important part of this, as dog handlers generally have a reputation of being very committed to their work.

The latest development in the field of MWDs in Norway is the use of dogs to detect IEDs along routes and possible axes of approach. This is an important contribution to force protection and the ability to operate safely.

Another development is using dogs to search for unexploded objects (UXOs) and duds in military live-firing ranges. There are several ranges that will be decommissioned, and these have to be cleared of any remnants of the military activity. At present this is being tested, but there seems to be very good prospects for using the dogs in areas that are difficult to clear by traditional means.

The NAF also cooperates with the Norwegian Defence Research Establishment (FFI) in developing command, control and communication (C3) equipment to be used on dogs. This includes a two-way voice and tone communications system and a high-definition video camera capable of streaming live video to a control unit operated by the dog handler. The system will make it possible to guide the dog from a safe distance, and also to do this in a covert manner, giving tactical advantages. The system should be able to be used on all categories of MWDs when it is operational. The MWDs have a natural place in the NAF; although the number of dogs and handlers is relatively small their effectiveness is greatly felt due to the quality and commitment of both.

SWEDEN

The first official document found in Sweden's War Archive describing the Swedish Armed Forces' (SAF's) working dogs is dated in the year 1897. It was written by a Lt Col Gustaf Trönnberg on behalf of the Royal Swedish Academy of War Sciences. It was a kind of report telling what the regulations could look like for the SAF. The document references other nation's war dogs and history, particularly how the ancient Greeks and Romans used their dogs for military purposes.

The text recommended that Sweden develop three criteria for war dogs:

- The dog should as a scout run in front of or alongside the marching patrol or unit and alert all that is suspicious.
- The dog should be used in reconnaissance companies and advanced parties. The dog should be sent out ahead of the troop and by the use of hand signals be called back. If there is anything suspicious out there the dog should alert to the handler.
- The third type of dog should be used as a messenger. In all cases the dog's work should be performed quietly without any barking.

In 1905 Lt B:son Lilliehök founded an organisation for medic (rescue) dogs. This organisation trained medic dogs over a period of two years. At this time the opinion was that the collie was the best breed for this purpose. Training trials were conducted at the maintenance and supply regiments in the towns of Örebro, Sala and Skövde between 1911 and 1914. This organisation was the embryo of today's Swedish Working dog Association that had its peak with over 65,000 members in the mid 1980s.

Lt Col Trönnberg was conducting military dog trials with the Västernorrland Regiment in the town of Sollefteå when World War I started and the armed forces had to stop the trials due to lack of finances.

One of the main reasons for using dogs in the armed forces for pulling or pack work was economics. It was expensive to contract horses in Sweden for all military duties. Dogs were smaller and didn't eat as much, or require big stables.

The long-term history starts with a man named Einar Edström, the founder of the Army Dog Centre in Sweden. Edström's military activities were in Sollefteå region (the northern part of Sweden). He raised his own breeding dogs for hunting, authored dog and hunting books, and developed the Swedish *seegebaden* (dog sled), among other things.

From 1911 to 1913 Einar Edström did service in the Västernorrlands Regiment. During this time he participated in trials conducted by Lt Col Trönnberg. The aim of the trials was to see how messenger dogs and draught dogs performed in the army. This was the time when he solidly established interest for working dogs in the military system. In 1936, by a royal proclamation, Major Edström founded the Army Dog Centre.

In 1942 there was an army dog instruction outlining what type of dogs would be trained for the SAF. The types were:

- communication dogs, messenger dogs and also dogs that helped pull out the communications lines between units—messenger dog's working criteria: run the distance by memory or track a natural or an artificial scent, and speed 4-6 kilometres (2.3-3.5 miles) per minute, the normal distance was 2-3 kilometres (1-2 miles); a good dog would run 5 kilometres (3 miles) or longer
- guard and patrol dogs
- dogs for field police work
- dogs for transportation duties.
- medic (search) dog—the medic dog actually founded the combat and search techniques for future tracking dogs

All of the dog types below were actually trained, though not in 1942 (the first mine detection dog was operational in 1949):

- gas dog
- gogs for the parachute services
- cadaver dogs
- mine detection dogs
- bomb detection dogs
- narcotic dogs
- storm dogs—dogs that were trained to run out in the terrain following a whistle sound that was created by special ammunition used in signal pistols. The dog dragged a weapon like a Bangalore torpedo. The purpose to get a mine-free path; this usually ended up in a one-way mission.

In 1946 the era of the communication dog was over, as more and more radios were introduced into the army. By this time automobiles also started to take over more and more of the pulling duties in the armed forces.

From the 1950s to the beginning of the 1980s dogs were mostly used for field police duties and patrol dogs at air bases for asset protection. Patrol dogs were also used in the UN missions Sweden participated in, such as Gaza, Sinai and the Congo.

At the beginning of the 1980s the Swedish Air Force changed the whole philosophy on how the ground defence forces should be used. There was a great development in combat techniques and how they should be organised. The choice of weapons for the ground defence elite ranger platoons included military working dogs.

Swedish Armed Forces Dog Instruction Centre (SAFDIC)

The Life Guards provide dog teams for regular armed forces units. Swedish Armed Forces Dog Instruction Centre (SAFDIC) raises and trains sniffer dogs to find weapons and explosives, and guard dogs for security. Along with their handlers, dogs are trained for rapid response missions, both nationally and internationally. SAFDIC is based outside Märsta, 50 kilometres (30 miles) north of Stockholm. The military dog breeding station is in Sollefteå.

SAFDIC's responsibilities include:
- representation of the dog working service
- procurement of dogs for the armed forces
- training of working dog personnel
- development of working dogs within the service
- production of arms and explosives sniffer dogs, and guard dogs
- rules and regulations for the dogs working within the service
- coordination of working dog services within the armed forces
- coordination with other government authorities

SAFDIC is the leading body for working dog services within the armed forces. SAFDIC supplies working dogs to the different units and is responsible for ensuring all dogs meet the exacting demands. SAFDIC has both career officer and civilian personnel, all with differing dog-related backgrounds.

Home Guard

The Swedish Home Guard (*Hemvärnet*) is a part of the SAF. The Home Guard consists of local defence units under the leadership of the armed forces, as well as 23 national auxiliary defence organisations. The Home Guard could be regarded as the equivalent of a fully government-controlled and sponsored version of the American state defense forces under the command of local army regiments.

Training focuses on guard duties and weapons proficiency. In peacetime the Home Guard's main task is to help with search and rescue operations and to provide assistance to civil society in cases of severe emergencies, such as natural disasters. Home Guard MWDs are used as sensor systems, usually two for every platoon. The animals are issued and trained by one of the national auxiliary defence organisations.

Mine Detection Dogs
Sweden has a long association with MDDs. They began during World War II and continue today in United Nations operations around the world as a leader in this field.
- 1944 the first MDD trials began
- 1951 the first operational live search
- 1950–60 Sinai and Gaza
- 1958 organising the army mine dog units
- mid-1980s, Lebanon (Kuwait just one month)
- 1994 Mine dog use closed down within SAF; technical systems were supposed to take over
- 1995 SAF trains Norway armed forces and US forces in MDD operations
- 1996 MDD squad sent to Bosnia
- 1997 Sweden cooperation with International Development Agency, Cambodia Mine Action Centre
- 1998 Operation MINURSO, Western Sahara, MDDs deployed
- 2003 Laos UXO MDD trials for humanitarian purposes

One method of operating MDDs is to send a dog forward off-leash down a designated lane to be cleared and searched. Upon locating a mine the MDD will make a passive response, and an engineer will go forward to make the mine safe. Another method of deploying MDD teams is from the safety of armoured protection vehicles. Swedish MDDs are taught to run well ahead of the vehicle along the intended route to be searched.

Today every service branch has its own anti-sabotage units. The air force has *Flygbasjägarna* (Swedish Air Force Rangers, SAFR), the army has *Militärpolisjägarna* (Military Police Rangers) and now the navy has *Bassäk* (Naval Counter SOF-Unit).

Navy MWD

A naval counter-special operations forces (SOF) unit company consists of 133 men and 12 dogs, one command and logistics platoon, two *SäkJakt* (Counter-SOF Ranger) platoons and two *Säkbevakning* (Counter SOF Guard) platoons. They can, with their own vehicles or in small fast boats, move anywhere they are needed. Concealed transports can be conducted with canoes or special swimmer equipment. One *SäkJakt* unit consist of four soldiers and one dog: a squad leader, armed with an AK5 and M203 (AK5C); a dog handler, armed with an AK5; a support man, armed with a KSP M/90; and a medic, armed with an AK5B.

The navy started its dog program in 1991–92. Learning from the army and the air force, they had a system where their dogs were used to search the small islands in the Swedish archipelago both on land and also from small boats and canoes. The main purpose for all these units was actually to act and perform operations to ensure that sabotage groups couldn't succeed in hitting assets.

During this period, there was a huge amount of research and development within the military dog organisation, with new techniques introduced:
- dogs being trained to detect scuba divers under water
- dogs being trained to detect explosives under water
- methods being developed for getting dogs out from chemical, biological, radiological and nuclear (CBRN) contaminated areas
- how to search for specific things that could be connected to persons
- combat techniques being developed so the dog could be used in 'silent attacks' where there is no visual contact before starting the attack movement
- explosive and weapons search methods being developed

• different methods being developed on searching mines, long leash, short leash methods for mine rescue teams, running in front of vehicles as security measure for avoiding anti-tank mines etc.

One threat against naval bases that is difficult to prevent is stealth operations carried out by an enemy's elite special forces units. To face these threats, the *Bassäkerhetskompaniet-Bassäk* (Naval Counter SOF Unit) was formed, specially equipped and trained to fulfil its mission of protecting naval bases against enemy special forces. The MWDs in this unit swim out from shore to detect enemy divers in the water.

Swedish Air Force Rangers

Prior to World War II, the tactic of the Swedish Air Force was to spread out air bases as much as possible so that they couldn't be bombed by the Soviet Union's air force in one wave. One of the criteria was also that fighter planes could take off and land from normal infrastructure roads. On each such air base there would be six close protection ground defence platoons and two air base ranger platoons.

Certain objects in this vicinity of air bases, such as vital roads and bridges, were also to be protected by the home guard with trained dogs.

In total, each air base housed six close protection platoons with eight dogs in each platoon, and two air base rangers platoons with eight dogs in each platoon.

So each air base had at least 64 dogs in service for the war organisation. At this time there were 32 air bases in Sweden. The system and methods are still the same today but on a much smaller scale. Today Sweden has only five air bases left and the armed forces are decreasing.

In total, the SAF had more than 4,000 dogs in its World War II establishment. In peacetime this has been reduced to approximately 1,000 dogs that are owned by the armed forces. There was also substantial cooperation with the Swedish working dog association where defence contracted over 3,000 dogs to serve during emergencies. Some of the people from the working dog association were also contracted to be a part of the war organisation, in case of a Russian invasion.

The SAFR (*Flygbasjägarna*) patrols are a qualitative unit with unique abilities not found elsewhere in the SAR. Their major tasks—reconnaissance, and combat search and rescue—neutralise any threat against grounded aviation, air force bases and support elements. The dog is the most important member of a patrol. It is used as a sensor to detect enemy forces, or else to escape contact with the enemy. These trained dogs can track human activity over a vast area.

The SAFR was created in 1983 to guard dispersed Swedish aircraft in the event of war. Upon a threat warning, all available aircraft leave their fixed airfields and disperse to mini-bases (in some cases nothing more than specially widened roadways with camouflaged, pre-positioned refuelling and armament supplies), making them less vulnerable to enemy air attacks. Guarding these sites are platoon-size ranger units, whose task is to search for and eliminate enemy saboteurs. The SAFR make extensive use of dogs and electronic sensors to locate enemy forces.

Denmark

Specialist units of MWDs belong to the air force. The MWD is a brand new unit in the Combat Support Wing and they are tasked to provide support to the Military Police and security forces. This is a role that gives a completely different type of sharp edge for the air force dog handlers than they would otherwise have been accustomed to. Prior to this MWDs were simple guard dogs designed to statically protect key facilities.

MWDs are placed under several tests prior to becoming operational. One of them is called the Defence *Mønstringsprøver*, which is a series of operational trials. These tests must be passed every year for the dog to remain operational. Dog handlers themselves must also pass a physical examination every year. The job requires handlers to be in good physical condition, not least to be able to follow the dog's pace. General fitness training is completed every day to meet these requirements.

The dogs are specially trained in search and tracking tasks. With their sensitive noses they can find everything from the most invisible trail of blood, to people hiding in dense scrub. Escape and evasion training is given to the *Frømand* Corps by the dog section. There are many who think they can fool the dog by walking in big arcs or by going into a river but it does not work.

Dogs are used by the regular armed forces in Denmark for activities such as patrol and tracking. It is in the field of sled dog operations however that Denmark is best known for its part in operation Sirius.

Sirius is a highly appropriate reference to the Dog Star (Sirius being the brightest star in the constellation Canis Major).

Slædepatuljen translates as 'sled patrol'. These units date back to World War II when the Danish military patrolled the Greenland icecap hunting for any hidden German meteorological reporting stations.

From among the *Frømandskorpset* (Danish military volunteers) are selected the personnel of one of the most extraordinary armed units— *Slæde-patuljen Sirius* (or sled patrol). Using dogsleds and the simplest of equipment, Sirius patrols cover all of north-eastern Greenland.

In the brief Arctic summer, kayaks are used to skirt the coastline. The rest of the year, Sirius patrols criss-cross the Greenland icecap asserting Danish sovereignty.

Sirius

Denmark has avoided creating any situations that could appear militarily provocative to other nations. Therefore, until the 1950s, only weather and direction stations were established along Greenland's northeast coast. When the Marine Command suggested occupation of the coast, the first steps to organise the Sirius patrol were undertaken. The project was called Operation Resolut and members were recruited from officers in the Danish Defence Unit. Later, in 1952, the sled patrol Resolut was officially established and the headquarters was moved from Ella Ø to Daneborg. However, a Canadian weather station was already located at Resolute Bay so to prevent misunderstandings, the patrol was renamed to Sirius in 1953.

Sirius consists of fourteen soldiers. Twelve are stationed in the patrol at Daneborg and two are located at the Defence Guard in Mestersvig. In 1994 the patrol was placed under the control of the Admiral Danish Fleet.

Sirius' assignments were:
1. to maintain Danish sovereignty in north and northeast Greenland
2. police the Northeast Greenland National Park, which is the world's largest
3. conduct military surveillance over 160,000 square kilometres by dog sled

The main Sirius station is at Daneborg (74 degrees north) in northeast Greenland. Until 1974 there was a Danish civilian weather station at the same location. For four months in the spring and for two months in the autumn, six sled teams, consisting of two men, eleven dogs and one sled each, patrol north and northeast Greenland. In summer, about 65 depots are laid out by the patrol itself for the coming winter's sled journeys. Depot laying is carried out by cutters, planes and helicopters.

Early in autumn, the sled teams build their own sleds and fabricate all the bags and boxes to be used on the sled journey. When there is sufficient snow, or when fjord ice is thick enough, training trips are conducted. Real patrol journeys start in early November. An average day's march is approximately 30 kilometres (19 miles), but these vary greatly depending on conditions. Primarily the patrol overnights in tents, but there are 65 huts maintained for Sirius use.

From June to August of every year, any male officers or non-commissioned officers in Danish service between the ages of 20 and 30 can apply. Applicants are selected following several interviews and psychological tests. After selection for Sirius, students start preparation for their upcoming service in January. Preparation extends until 1 July, and around 20 July the Sirius men go to northeast Greenland. There they will serve for two continuous years.

The sled patrol is under command of the Admiral Danish Fleet stationed in Århus. From here the patrol is managed by the Patrol Branch North and Northeast Greenland (PNG), which is stationed at naval station Auderød (also a basic training station for sailors). People in active service in PNG are all former members of Sirius. In addition to the main field headquarters of Sirius is at Daneborg, there is a support station at Ella Ø in Kong Oscars Fjord (72 degrees north). This station is only active in summer, when four to six Sirius members live there and are busy laying out depots by boat.

During summer, various levels of Sirius members are present, including personnel who are about to return to Denmark after two years' service, those who have a year to go, and recently arrived men who are beginning their service. In addition, three or more people from PNG are present, helping with logistical activities during the short summer period.

In addition to the twelve men stationed at Daneborg, PNG has two former members of the patrol stationed at the former mining airport at Mestersvig (260 kilometres, 161 miles south of Daneborg). These two men are part of the Sirius surveillance and radio service and also maintain the airport runway and ten large buildings. During the summer, about 30 research and pleasure expeditions visit the national park. Each must obtain special permits from the Greenland government and Sirius controls them.

Sirius patrols the world's biggest national park with an operation area of 160,000 square kilometres (99,420 square miles, about three times the size of Denmark). During the 54 years that Sirius has been operational, more than 750,000 kilometres (466,000 miles) have been patrolled on dog sled. In the same period, cutters in association with depot lying have traversed more than 100,000 nautical miles.

Sirius is scheduled for one supply ship visit per year. However, two years of supplies are always maintained on hand because of the chance that the ship will not be able to navigate through coastal ice. About 30 tonnes of supplies are transported yearly to the 65 sled depots.

The average time of service for a Sirius dog is five years. Only those not run-out are allowed to live on after their fifth year, and in that case they are distributed between Station North, Danmarkshavn and Mestersvig.

Sirius breeds their own dogs. The optimal dog is shorthaired with erect ears, long-legged, with a weight between 40 and 50 kilograms (88 and 100 pounds). By the time a dog is retired it will likely have travelled more than 20,000 kilometres (12,400 miles) in a sled team.

Daneborg consists of 23 buildings. Sirius has four generators, each of which can deliver between 150 and 250 kilowatts. About 180,000 litres (47,500 gallons) of oil are consumed each year at the station. The oil, along with 300 tonnes of supplies, is transported by ship from Denmark. Christmas presents are dropped by parachute at full moon in December.

Sirius helps support scientific investigations through such activities as animal and bird censuses and banding. Logistical support is also often provided for scientific expeditions in the area.

Sledding and Patrolling

Sirius sled dogs originally come from the Greenlandic dog, but through careful crossbreeding, Sirius has produced a heavier and stronger dog. Puppies are allowed to roam around on their own until they reach their 'teen' years, when they are chained up with the other dogs, ready to start sledding when the autumn journey starts.

The sled is built by the patrol members; one week is set aside per team. This is so that any officer will be able to fix his sled if it breaks on patrol. The sled runners are made of waterproof plywood or ash wood, which are reinforced with 15mm of nylon band on the sliding band, and the floorboards are made of unknotted ash wood. Everything is tied together with nylon line, so that the sled can move more over rugged terrain and remain flexible. Each sled weighs about 80 kilograms (17 pounds) and can carry a load of up to 400 kilograms (880 pounds). Loaded sledges are pulled by 11 dogs, each of which weighs from 35-50 kilograms (70-100 pounds).

Besides building sleds, sled drivers also fabricate harnesses, traces, dog chains, necklaces, bags, boxes and other equipment, which is individual for each sled. The conditions in the patrols' remote surveillance area are harsh and unforgiving: people patrolling here must always be very alert. There are extremely low winter temperatures, storms with the strength of a hurricane and great amounts of snow. In addition, polar bear, musk oxen and wolves need to be taken seriously at all times. This is why a sled team is always made up of a new and an old Sirius member. In that way the old can train the new to act correctly under all circumstances.

Sirius men must be able to drive dogs in all kinds of weather; from deep snow to smooth ice, over 10-15-metre (33-49 feet) high ice packs, places with no snow or ice, through frozen rivers and passes with rises and falls of 20-30 per cent. The visibility varies from complete white-out conditions, where there is only a compass or GPS for navigation, to more than 100 kilometres (62 miles), where a 1:1,000,000 scale map gives a brilliant view.

Following a day of patrol, each Sirius team member must prepare for the night by erecting a tent and carefully stowing all gear, such as radio, sleeping bags, food supplies, Primus and clothes. The dogs must be fed and everything secured. When sleeping in a tent, the team must also construct a snow bank around the tent for security against stormy weather. During the night, the dogs must be checked several times, so when the team has been sledging the whole day (six-ten hours) they really need all the sleep they can get. However this must follow cooking meals, radio communications with the base, diary writing and patrol view reporting.

A sled team generally drives about 4,000 kilometres (2,485 miles) in a season. In the 54 years of Sirius operation, more than 750,000 kilometres

(466,000 miles) have been sledded, which is more than sixteen times around Earth's equator! More than 260 sled drivers have served two years in this honoured and historic organisation.

FINLAND

Veterinarian Johan Brüningen demanded a program for war dogs after Finland became independent in 1918. The first Finnish war dogs were used during the Trip of Aunus in 1919. (The Trip of Aunus was an attempt by Finnish volunteers to conquer some parts of Eastern-Karelia and annex them to Finland. This happened in 1919, during the Russian civilian war.) Captain V Kaski delivered a group of medication dogs to the frontline. The group included five men and four dogs.

Kaski was also the founder of *Suomen Armeijakoirayhdistys ry* (Finnish Military Dog Association). The association was founded in 1921, and in the same year the first issues of war dog magazine *Sotakoira* were published.

Actual war dog activity in Finnish defence forces started when the Danish army donated two dogs, Björn (male) and Asta (female) in 1923. The first war dog kennels were founded in 1924. At that time, the defence forces had 20-30 dogs. Dogs were trained to be messenger dogs (dogs carrying messages in special collar from point A to point B) and medication dogs (*sanitär-hunden*). Civil guards also used dogs, until the guards were abolished after World War II.

Winter War 1939-1940
Before the Winter War all dogs were trained to be messenger dogs, and this was the main purpose for dogs during the Winter War. Dogs used in the war were donated by individuals and war dogs were trained by civil guards. The dogs were not particularly useful during the war, due to a lack of good handlers. Most handlers were ordered to the task and were not very motivated. Most of the dogs were untrained, or had had only a quick training period.

Winter 1939-40 was very cold, with a lot of snow, and there were a lot of problems using the messenger dogs because of the weather. In February 1940 the soldiers noticed a need for tracking dogs. An urgent message was sent to Hämeenlinna (a city in Finland) to start training approximately 50 tracking dogs for the frontline. The dogs were to be used in a reconnaissance role against the Russian partisans. The Finnish army had about 100 dogs in use during the Winter War.

The Continuation War 1941-1944

Dogs were used in patrolling, tracking and guarding. Messenger dogs were no longer used due to better technical communication systems. Patrol dogs were trained for tracking, which included locating mines and the wires of booby traps. Dogs were also supposed to expose a hiding person (in an ambush). During the Continuation War, Russian prisoners of war were used in dog training. Prisoners who volunteered to be a target person got extra portions of food.

In 1942 the army kennels were asked to increase the number of tracking dogs. They were used for tracking down enemies, reconnaissance parachutists and partisans.

Close to the Finnish border, in the area of Uhtua, was one of the biggest training centres of the Russian partisans. The Russian partisans were very active during the Positions War, especially in autumn 1943. The dogs that were used in the long distance patrols didn't give good results. The short time the dogs and their handlers had for training was thought to be the main reason; their course only lasted one week. On the long-distance patrols the dogs got tired, made noise and also chased game. The patrol leaders' mistrust for using dogs was also a reason why the handler wasn't always allowed to come along. Sometimes a dog had to be put down for endangering the patrols by making noise. Even so, by 1944 the Finnish army had the most dogs in the war, with more than 600 dogs in use.

Most dogs were used by the army group of Aunus, coast brigade of Ääninen and the Third Army group.

POW Camps

Finnish POW camps had at most 80 dogs in use. At first they used guard dogs only, but due to many attempts to escape they wanted to change their guard dogs to tracking dogs.

The Finnish army didn't have any separate dog groups. The main rule was that the dog handler and his dog were sent from the Third Army especially for the term needed. The shortage of good and voluntary dog handlers was problematic. Before the war, working and obedience dog clubs were popular in Finland. The working and obedience dog sport was designed only for national defensive purposes. When this kind of hobbyist got a war dog to train and guide, the results were good.

One such dog sports champion attached to the Third Army group was Sgt Niilo Toivonen, who trained dogs long before the war. The Academy of War Dogs in Hämeenlinna was closed down on 30 November 1944, and those dogs in its custody were reassigned to the border guard. Some of these dogs continued in Lapland conducting de-mining tasks till 1945.

Important Dates
- 1946: Finnish Defence Forces restarted their dog function.
- 1960: The systematic breeding function of the Finnish army and its kennel began.
- 1961: Mine dogs' training began, finishing in 1969.
- 1966: The Finnish army started its own breeding kennels. The same year the first Finnish dogs went to work with UN troops at Sinai.
- 1991: The first arms and explosive search (AES) dog and handler were trained in co-operation with the Finnish Police Academy.
- 1998: Defence forces start training AES dogs and handlers.
- 2002: Defence forces start training drug dogs and handlers.

Today
Military dogs are used during peacetime as assistants the Military Police (MP). Dogs are also used in teaching conscripts to become dog handlers. A few MP

dogs are being used in peacekeeping missions in Kosovo (KFOR) where they are used for patrolling and searching for explosives, arms and drugs.

Types of Military Dogs in Use

Patrol dogs are used by the MP. Their basic training includes tracking, obedience and protection. Some of these dogs are trained to also be AES or drug detection dogs. Patrol dogs are trained by the conscripts. The basic training for them includes tracking and obedience. Some of these dogs are trained for protection. Dog training given to the conscripts aims to meet MP standards during war or crisis. AES dogs are trained at the artillery brigade in Niinisalo and Kainuun Prikaati to search for explosives and arms and their components. Most dogs that are trained for AES are so-called combined dogs (trained to bite as well as search). These dogs also work with their handler as MP patrol dogs. Drug detection dogs are trained to search for narcotics and related equipment, and usually also work as MP patrol dogs.

The centre of Finnish military dog activity is Niinisalo, Artillery Brigade. The War Dog Department, which is part of the Artillery Brigade, acquires, tests and verifies all dogs intended for military use and arranges war dog training courses. The War Dog Department trains the conscripts to act as dog handlers in MP companies.

At the moment Finland has around 198 operational dogs in the roles of patrol, narcotic and explosive detection, water and cadaver search, and a new accelerant-detection dog project. The Finnish Police Dog Association (*Suomen Polisikoirakunioni R.Y.*) was founded in 1965 and has about 240 members and an executive committee with members from twelve districts. Finnish police dogs can be used by the military for internal operations and in time of war.

Patrol work in Arctic conditions is a vital part of Finland's MWD training program. Dogs are sometimes carried in a small sled, pulled by the handler on skis: a reverse on the usual image of the husky hauling a human.

Europe

France

Of all the Allies during World War I, the French used more dogs and in the most ways. The French War Dog Service was established shortly after the beginning of World War I in 1914, and its success was largely due to the untiring efforts of Sgt Paul Megnin, who later became chief of the service. Even though the French military had used sentry dogs as early as the 18th century, Sgt Megnin still had to overcome the prejudices of commanders who couldn't understand how to use the dogs tactically in the war zone.

The French War Dog Service organised two kennels near Paris and a third in Normandy for the training of dogs, and a fourth was being contemplated at the time the Armistice was signed in 1918. As soon as the four-footed defenders had completed their education the handlers were sent to the school at Satory for an eight-day course in dog handling. During this time they became thoroughly acquainted with the particular animals with which they were to work at the front.

Besides using auxiliary sentry dogs, the French also had what they called enclosure dogs. These were simply efficient watchdogs who were set free at night inside an enclosed area, such as a factory yard. Used mainly by the French Minister of Armament, training of these dogs lasted from ten days to two weeks. Tracker dogs were trained for at least three months. Pack and driving dogs (these were large powerful breeds not qualified for other army work) were used for pulling machine guns, mortar and supply carts and as pack dogs. The French messenger dogs were divided into two classes:

estafettes who were trained to run with a message from one point to another, and the liaison dogs, trained to also return with an answer to the message.

The French started World War II with considerable numbers of war dogs; however, due to France's quick defeat they did not get a chance to prove themselves in operational service. Many French war dogs were taken over by the occupation troops and used as guard dogs, some, no doubt, against their old masters.

Very little is known about France's dogs of war today, as all information concerning them is strictly classified. However, in 1991 during the Gulf War, French forces included a division of 1,177 highly trained canines. The air force dogs, most of them German shepherds, served as 'mobile radars' by patrolling the grounds near French Jaguar fighter planes, according to Alain Colorado, commander of the dog division. These numbers are impressive when compared to the United States' 80 canine teams in theatre. It is thought that France probably has the largest number of war dogs in use today of any country other than Israel, Colombia and the United States.

In France today, military working dogs (MWDs) are used by all armed forces, including the French Foreign Legion and their national police (GIGN). About 3,400 French troops are in Afghanistan, Tajikistan, Kyrgyzstan, and in the Indian Ocean as part of NATO's International Security Assistance Force (ISAF) and Operation Enduring Freedom (OEF). Among these troops, 2,800 are deployed in Afghanistan. France currently has 32 teams of dog handlers in foreign missions in six different areas: Lebanon, Gabon, Guyana, Cote D'Ivoire, Kosovo and Kabul Province.

The army has a canine unit: the 132nd Battalion Canine (132nd CTAB), based in Suippes in Marne (51). This particular regiment trains around 250 dogs every year for service in the army, and also supplies MWDs to the air force and navy. 2007 marked the official ceremony connecting the 132nd Battalion of the Canine Army (132nd BCAT) to the engineer brigade. The 132nd Battalion of the Canine Army specialises in the use of handlers and dogs in the areas of security, response and detection (weapons and explosives). It has the largest military kennel in Europe, with a capacity of nearly 700 dogs.

Its flag bears the motto '*un contre huit*' ('one against eight') in the colours of the Croix de Guerre. It honours a dual parentage: that of the 132nd Infantry Regiment, which served during the French Revolution, through the Empire and during the two world wars, and that of the training centre of the 54th Veterinary Group and 24th Veterinary Group, which has retained the expertise for canine treatment in the Military. This dual affiliation makes the 132nd BCAT unique; its purpose is to provide expertise on the operational use of MWD teams in the support of French ground forces.

The composition of the battalion which is attached to the command area of Metz is subject to the army for all matters concerning doctrine. The structure of the regiment consists of five companies:

• three companies of intervention dog teams (these are patrol dogs which are seen out in front of an infantry section): one in Saint-Christol one in Vaucluse and the other in Biscarrosse

• one company for training and supporting dog teams, handlers, dog managers and dog technicians at all levels

• one company for the support and logistics of all things dog, such as purchase, delivery, management, veterinary care and infrastructure

General initial training for the dogs is over nine weeks. Initial training of specialty dog handling is five weeks. Dog handlers in the section specialise as tracker and patrol (intervention) or explosives search (EOD).

The French battalion (BATFRA) from the Belvédère camp carries out a synchronised patrol each week, with troops from the Notting Hill camp and the Serbian army, through remote villages settled along the north of Kosovo's administrative border. These patrols aim to prevent smuggling and any illegal activity along the border. Relations between Kosovo Force (KFOR) troops and armed forces from neighbouring countries are very important in the ability to fight efficiently against this criminal action. MWDs, as usual, lead the way, and are used to both detect the enemy and search for explosives. With 2,000 soldiers deployed in Kosovo, France contributes a lot to KFOR and represents the third strongest contingent after Germany and Italy. French forces are mainly deployed within the MNTF-N (Multinational Task Force-North).

KFOR is the second most important NATO-led operation after Afghanistan. France took command of the operation for a year from September 2007. French MWD teams in Kosovo man vehicle checkpoints, searching for explosives and arms. A secondary role of dog teams is to support KFOR civilian police forces in crowd control operations.

The French battalion in Afghanistan carries out stability and security operations in the areas it is entrusted with. Units of the BATFRA take both preventative and deterrent actions. They perform daily patrols–by foot and vehicle–among the Afghan population, conducting joint checkpoints in liaison with the Afghan police and monitoring surrounding hot spots such as the airport.

French MWD teams patrol the perimeter of the airfield and rural and urban areas as part of an infantry patrol squad. They aim to hinder terrorist actions and hamper the rebels' movements, while also reassuring the population. The BATFRA also contributes to the security of the population by recovering and destroying unexploded munitions, especially shells and landmines. The BATFRA musters about 800 military personnel. Engineer dog team detachments beef up the French infantry companies. The dogs are effectively trained to search for both weapons and explosive devices.

During Operation Bloodhound in June 2009 at Uzbin in the district of Surobi, a specialised operational search (FOS) team located five caches of weapons and ammunition that contained small arms, grenades and 160 rounds of various types. These could be used to make road side improvised explosive devices (IEDs), which constitute the most serious threat to military and civilian populations.

The specialised operational search team consists of dog teams from the air commandos and two EOD divers from a navy minesweeper. The main body, consisting of soldiers from the 17th Parachute Engineer Regiment of the army, contains several elite sub-units, which are grouped into two platoons within the support company. The first is the *Neutralization et Destruction des Explosifs* (NEDEX) section which performs EOD duties for the unit, including recently providing EOD teams to support a number of combat operations in both Africa and Europe. The second unit is *Unite Cynophile* (Dog Unit), which uses specially trained dogs to detect explosives.

French soldiers with military working dogs from the United Nations Interim Forces in Lebanon (UNIFIL) took part in a medal parade held ahead of a future troop rotation at their base in the southern Lebanese town of Tireh, near the border with Israel, on 15 September 2009. With a 1,600-strong force of 'blue helmets', France is the second largest contributor to UNIFIL, beefed up after the UN-brokered truce between Lebanon and Hezbollah took effect in August 2006. According to a UNIFIL statement released on 15 September 2009, France has lost 28 soldiers during service in Lebanon since it started sending peacekeeping troops to the east Mediterranean country in 1978.

Military Veterinarians

Military veterinarians perform various missions in France and overseas operations. They include veterinary public health (hygiene and food safety), and treatment and prevention of animal diseases of both military and civilian animals. In Kabul, French military veterinarians are responsible for the health of 30 MWDs and for the French, Belgian and American MWDs at the detachments in Croatia. In the French base camp named Warehouse, the vets check drinking water systems and sanitation systems daily, as well as being responsible for decontamination of equipment to prevent transmittable diseases.

French Gendarmie

The (French) National Gendarmerie has a canine unit called the National Centre for Canine Section of the Gendarmerie (CNICG), established in December 1945 and located in Gramat. The gendarmerie operates approximately 41 groups of dog teams totalling 645 dogs.

Within the French Gendarmerie is the National Gendarmerie Intervention Group, commonly abbreviated to GIGN (*Groupe d'Intervention de la Gendarmerie Nationale*). This is an elite counter-terrorism and hostage rescue unit that is part of the Military Police, rather than the civilian police.

The GIGN is divided into a command cell, an administrative group, four operational troops of twenty, an operational support troop including specialists in negotiation, breaching, intelligence, communications, marksmanship, and MWD teams.

Air Force

The French Air Force regularly tests its canine units with an annual five-day challenge held at Air Base Orleans at Sicut Aquila. Each air commando team is composed of three Commandos and a dog handler. The program includes shooting events day and night, orienteering and the highlight of the challenge: a 'technical commando' course, which is a timed race punctuated by various obstacles over a distance of 5.8 kilometres (3.6 miles). Participants crawl, climb, descend rope zip lines and cross water obstacles.

The air force has twenty dog teams specialised in EOD. The dogs are responsible for the detection of explosives or hazardous substances on airplanes and in airport zones. Recently, Air Force Base 102 'Captain Guynemer' Dijon was strengthened by additional dog teams. They were used for missions involving search and detection of suspicious packages and explosives in aircraft and vehicles, and people.

The Elite of the Elite

Camp Raff, home of the 2nd REP French Foreign Legion in Corsica, is surrounded by barbed wire and patrolled by dog handlers with their *chiens de guerre* (war dogs). The four-legged legionnaires are qualified for scouting, tracking, searching for explosives and attack functions. Twenty-five male German shepherd and Belgian malinois dogs are brought from several European Countries and selected for their aggression and intelligence between twelve to eighteen months of age.

The intensive training has taught the dogs to bark or attack only when ordered. Any intruder foolish enough to enter the camp will be detected and apprehended by these alert legionnaires. In camp they function predominantly during darkness to best utilise their night vision capabilities. In the field they operate in advance of the troops.

In 1994 the dog platoon was part of the 1st Company. They are present during all the company's activities, including live-fire exercises, flights and street-fighting operations: the company's specialty. A recent demo showed two dogs supporting a platoon attacking a fortified dwellings. A special sling has been designed to allow the dogs to travel on the back of the handler as they rappel down the sheer face of a mountain or building for fast insertion methods. A similar harness enables the dogs to be parachuted into live operational drop zones or deployed via helicopter insertion through jungle canopy, such as that found in French Guyana.

The French Foreign Legion contingent in Afghanistan has a secret weapon against the insurgents' homemade bombs, the Belgian malinois. These dogs are trained to sniff rudimentary explosives and have enabled the Legion to discover dozens of caches of weapons and roadside bombs. These roadside bombs require very little technology and have no metal parts or traditional explosives, making them virtually undetectable by the usual clearance equipment. The malinois accompanying the French Foreign Legion in the area of Torah are able to detect not only conventional explosives, but also handmade rustic ordnance compounds, which the Taliban are resorting to more and more.

GERMANY

The Imperial German staff began to develop war dog breeds during the latter years of the 19th century. Principles and practices established then and early on in the next century proved so sound that they became the standard for the rest of the world.

Beginning in the late 1860s, village clubs were established throughout Germany for the breeding and training of dogs for war. They were subsidised by the Imperial Prussian Army. In 1884 the general staff established the world's very first Military War Dog School, at Lechernich near Berlin, and initially trained dogs as sentries and messengers. They were also the first to introduce the Red Cross dog; their school's head trainer, Herr von Bungartz, trained units of dogs who wore saddlebags containing medical supplies to search for the wounded on a field of battle.

During the Herrero Campaign (1904-1907) in German West Africa, 60 war dogs were deployed to the armies. Time and again these dogs saved the troops from enemy ambushes in the dense terrain.

When hostilities were declared in August 1914 the German army had 6,000 trained war dogs ready for action. In addition, the army was able to call on a reserve pool of trained dogs from the German police force.

Ambulance dogs, referred to as sanitary dogs (*sanitätshunde*), were able to distinguish between the dead and the injured; the former they left untouched. The English and French armies found it impossible to employ ambulance dogs on the Western Front during the late war, but the German army seems to have done so, especially during the Russian retreat on the Eastern Front, with conspicuous success. It is officially recorded that thousands of German soldiers owed their lives to ambulance dogs.

Messenger dogs also constituted an acknowledged part of the organisation of the German Army. An infantry regiment was allocated a maximum of twelve dogs, while a battalion might have six. The allocations were made by the Messenger Dog Section (*Meldehundstaffel*) at the Army Headquarters. The breeds chiefly employed for message-carrying work were German shepherds, Dobermans, Airedale terriers and Rottweilers. The Germans, unlike the British, employed the dogs on the double-journey liaison principle: that is, with two handlers per dog.

At the end of World War I some German dogs were taken over by the Allies for use and breeding. Many more, however, were destroyed, as following the German defeat military restrictions and the overall economy could not sustain anywhere near previous peacetime numbers. However, Germany under Hilter ignored the Versailles Treaty and military numbers were slowly increased. With a restricted army of 100,000 men Germany found the war dog to be a great force multiplier. The Germans founded the military kennels at Frankfurt in 1934 and by 1939 had about 50,000 trained war dogs ready for use.

As German forces advanced into both Belgium and France, the Germans lost no time in seizing all suitable dogs and sending them back to Germany to be trained. Once trained, the dogs were drafted to army kennels; each army had one from which dogs were issued to the front-line troops. During World War II the German army made extensive use of war dogs in a variety of roles: some traditional, such as guarding airfields, railway heads and logistical areas against sabotage and commando-style attacks. They were also employed behind the lines to track down partisan groups and in the front lines as scout dogs. It also cannot be ignored that war dogs were put to some distasteful uses, such as in concentration camp guard employment. However, the very reason they were used in the latter role was they could be used as a terror weapon out of proportion to their numbers. One camp guard dog could in effect secure an area that might have required 50 soldiers, thus freeing up manpower to fight on the front. Such was the brutal use of some of these dogs, they left a negative opinion of war dogs that took several years to overcome.

During the Winter War, in the frozen desolate hinterland of the north, the German Sixth SS Mountain Division (Nord) was the only German military unit to have dogs as part of its official establishment. The dog section comprised three different groups of dogs: scout, messenger and sled dogs known as *Ziehhunden*. There were 30 men assigned to the dog section known as *Hunderfuhrer* or dog drivers. Their task included haulage of supplies to the front lines and evacuation of the wounded. There is no official estimate of their success, but one soldier's diary stated in 1943 that he and his dog evacuated more than 340 wounded troops from the front alone.

Dogs were not used in sled teams but often operated alone, or typically in a three-dog tandem harness between wooden shafts pulling a *pulkka*, or *akja:* a Finnish boat-like wooden sled.

The German Army Dog School

The German Army Dog School (*Diensthunde*) is located in Elm. It is Germany's only military dog school (*Hundeschule*). During the initial weeks the pups are socialised and develop a close bond with their new master. Previously, military dogs were purchased at an age of one to one and a half years. In order to meet strict selection criteria and growing demand, the school began its own breeding program in the autumn of 2003.

Not all four-legged candidates meet the high demands of military selection; only after a thorough examination of their health and character does training begin. The specific characteristics of different breeds are considered. While Belgian and German shepherds are versatile and used in most MWD roles, the labrador is especially favoured for the detection of mines.

All dogs are trained to passively signal the particular odour they are trained to locate, be it explosive or narcotics; they sit down and look towards the odour. Previously, sniffer dogs gave an active response by scratching or barking.

In 1996 the Federal Defense Force (*Bundeswehr*) was tasked with deployments abroad and found that the need for specialist dogs had increased significantly. Previously, dogs were trained in guard and police-type roles only (*Wachbegleithund*). Today, military dogs are also trained in one of several specialties. In 1999 there was a further addition to the training requirements; MWDs were to also have a mine detection capability during overseas operations.

In 1999 the decision was made that other army units, apart from Military Police (MP), would form dog units. In 2000, specialist dogs were deployed in Kosovo and the training of personal trackers dogs began.

The school for service dogs has its own modern animal clinic with everything a modern veterinary clinic requires, including two operating rooms, treatment rooms, dental facilities and a care and quarantine facility. Military veterinarians are also active in research and nutrition, testing dogs on their fitness for service.

German Parachute Battalions

Within all four German parachute battalions (*Fallschirmjäger* 313, 263, 373 and 261), the support companies maintain a canine platoon. While the German Army is predominantly made up of conscripts, 80 per cent of the elite *Fallschirmjäger* consists of longer-serving professionals.

The canine platoons were introduced in the airborne forces in the late 1990s as part of the specialisation of the paratroopers. A standard dog platoon can field 24 soldiers and is structured into two sections with nine dog handlers and dogs apiece. The platoon's special equipment includes air-portable cages for the dogs, dog trailers and all necessary kit for keeping the animals operational. Dog teams are usually deployed in teams of two with two handlers and two MWDs. In operations, one handler serves as a leader and cover man (without a dog) for the other dog handler.

The *Fallschirmjäger* employ two types of trained dogs: guard dogs and sniffer dogs. The guard dogs are trained to track down persons of interest and to detain them. They are employed to locate enemy fighters during arrest operations in an asymmetric conflict or their own troops during a rescue operation. They can also be employed with patrols, at checkpoints or on base security operations in order to provide the additional capabilities of their superior senses. During riot control operations they can be deployed to arrest ringleaders or to keep a violent mob at bay.

The sniffer dogs are trained to detect explosives, ammunition, weapons and certain chemicals. They can be employed during search operations or at vehicle checkpoints. Sniffer dogs are dual-trained and can also be employed as guard dogs.

Before a soldier becomes a dog handler, he is fully trained as an infantryman and has to complete a parachute course. All dog handlers are volunteers. Handlers and their dogs are trained for insertion by helicopter, including abseiling from the hovering craft.

In 2002 dog handlers from *Fallschirmjäger* Battalion 313 were successfully employed in Kabul to stop a group of rowdy Afghans who were trying to enter an already overcrowded football stadium. Through this action the dogs and their handlers prevented a mass panic and probably saved the lives of hundreds of people. Since then MWD handlers have had numerous deployments to Afghanistan as part of International Security Assistance Force (ISAF) contingent. In 2009 they saw action in Feyzabab.

Overseas Deployments

Currently German military working dogs are deployed in all German overseas operations. Since World War II German troops have not had many international tours of duty due to poor public opinion. Nowadays, the *Bundeswehr* are a regular partner in United Nations-led operations. Military dog handlers are in Afghanistan and the Balkans assisting in mine detection, explosive detection and general assistance to police operations. Wherever German soldiers are providing their services at home or abroad, there are members of the MP force with them.

German MP dog handlers, as part of KFOR in Kosovo, are used as base security, in general police support functions including riot control, tracking offenders, general deterrence and in specialist roles such as EOD. All Military Police dogs are versatile, trained in a variety of skills such as man-work, tracking, riot control, agility, search and a specialist detection role. In peacetime, MP dogs are used to patrol camps and installations within Germany and abroad, conduct patrols with Infantry units or work with local police forces. Other roles in wartime would include POW guarding.

A service dog handler in the MP force (all SNCOs) are full-time professionals, unlike most of the German Army which is based on conscription. MP dogs are well socialised due to their policing function and may have to work in the civilian, military and international communities. The MP is the only German army dog unit that operates narcotic detection dogs (NDD).

At the beginning of a career as a service dog in the Military Police, dogs attend puppy school during the first weeks of life. The puppies are shaped and socialised and build up a close bond with their new masters. Once mature, around eighteen months of age, the MP dog attends a three-month basic training course, then goes directly into the specialisation phase (narcotic detection or explosive detection) which is completed after approximately 21 weeks.

BELGIUM

Before the suspension of compulsory military service in 1991, which resulted in drying up the supply of reserves, MWDs were used in relatively small numbers. Since then, the realisation that one dog could replace up to 50 members of the reserves for guarding an area has caused the MWD program in Belgium to readily expand. Today Belgium uses more than 526 dog teams to guard vital infrastructure.

The Belgium army has a long tradition of using MWDs. During World War I the Belgium Army used large breeds to haul machine guns around the forward trenches. Some 200 Belgian and French dogs were evacuated with the troops from Dunkirk during World War II and served with the Allied forces.

MWDs have also been used by operational forces internationally in Belgian colonial wars in Africa where they were used both in the guarding of installations and colonial possessions, and as tracker dogs during anti-guerrilla operations. The Public Force (PF) was the official armed force for what is now the Democratic Republic of the Congo. An engineer's unit containing more than 12,100 men also possessed a large military dog unit.

Today, apart from the main role of security patrol duties, MWDs are being trained in Belgium to carry out various missions such as mine detection, locating aircrew after a crash or survivors during a natural disaster, and explosive detection dog (EDD) teams.

In the Air Component, fifteen explosive detection dogs security (EDD Sy) teams are currently working in international operations. The Air Component also includes tracking dogs.

The Unit Kennels Interforze (UCI) has been created to support the training and operational capability of military dogs. The UCI has a present structure of 31 soldiers who meet the welfare needs of service dogs. The training and daily inspections of MWDs are performed by the four kennels scattered all over the country. Treatments and vaccines are the responsibility of the veterinarians who are stationed at the canine clinic in Oud-Heverlee. The command of the UCI is also located in Oud-Heverlee and is responsible for the organisation and administration of staff and dogs.

In addition to meeting daily tasks there is a MWD response team of EDDs. These dogs are always ready to seek all kinds of explosives at short notice. In addition, this team conducts dog demonstrations given for the benefit of the public on most weekends of the summer months.

Competitions

Belgium holds MWD contests each year for both its own troops and international handlers to compete in.

The Master Guardian Dog contest in 2009 took place in Meerdaal. All up, 21 dog-guardian teams, selected for their performance during the year, participated. They took part in four different workshops. Each team was tested in the obedience class, shooting with dog, drill and detection patrol. At the end of the day the teams of Security K SUD were the winners.

The first International Inter Powers Kennels Stage Days Competition (EDDs) was organised in September 2009. The objective is to unify the EDD teams from different nations (Belgium, Germany, Netherlands, France, Luxembourg and United States) to work together and develop common practices with operating EDD. This competition enables handlers to enhance individual skills and share experiences with others.

The Directorate of Special Units (DSU) is the Belgian federal police's counter-terrorism unit. One team has six trained police dogs for detecting the presence of explosive materials or ammunition, the other one is the Disaster Victim Identification (DVI) team, which was created in 1978 after the Los Alfaques disaster. The administrative police Canine Support Group has 35 dog teams. Some dogs are trained to detect drugs, human remains, hormones or fire accelerants. About one-third are tracker dogs trained to find or identify living people. These teams are often deployed to earthquake areas to locate people trapped in collapsed buildings. The federal police's EDDs are attached to the CGSU special units.

Belgium has also had F-16s in Afghanistan to provide support to ISAF. During the stabilisation phase of the mission, the international military forces needed additional combat aircraft in southern Afghanistan. The presence of these fighters is necessary to ensure air support to ISAF troops when the situation demands.

Three dogs (two patrol and one explosive) deploy in a bimonthly role in Afghanistan to ensure the security of Kabul airport. This is a very challenging task; teams work seven days a week for two months. Each night, the dog handlers walk the line where the planes are parked from France, Netherlands and Belgium. Their mission during Operation Guardian Falcon is to detect intrusions and prevent acts of sabotage or destruction of aircraft and facilities, control and secure the operational area and the perimeter of the camp.

Another role in Afghanistan for the Belgian EDD is as part of the explosive ordnance disposal (EOD) team, whose mission is composed of three major parts: intervention in cases of plane crash at the airport or in the vicinity, removal of any dangerous munitions or IEDs if discovered on the Kabul airport and thirdly, to be ready as a reserve team for the entire area's Regional Command Capital in Kabul Province for the removal or destruction of IEDs. The two-man dog team is attached to the 11th Engineer Battalion from the UCI (Unit Kennels Interforze) to deal with EDD requirements such as vehicle checkpoint control of all trucks and tankers arriving at the base. They also provide support for all EOD interventions, conducting sweeps and searches as required.

Austria

In 1955 Austria declared its everlasting neutrality and made neutrality a constitutional law. The main constitutional tasks of today's Austrian military are to maintain order and security inside the country and to render assistance in the case of natural catastrophes and disasters of exceptional magnitude. MWD teams have been used in the search and rescue role in such cases.

The Austrian Military Police (MP) is the branch within the Austrian armed forces tasked with law enforcement and the protection of military events and Austrian armed forces property.

The MP is also tasked with operations with MWDs. Becoming a dog handler in Austria is a long and difficult process. Before admission to the MP selection course, every candidate has to successfully complete basic training 1, 2 and 3, as well as the corporals' course. Having passed this selection course, the candidate is admitted to the first semester of the non-commission officer (NCO) training course at the NCO Academy. During the second semester the candidate starts MP basic training at the Training Division of the Military Police Command in Vienna. Then, after the successful completion of this course, the candidate becomes a member of the MP. Only after all this is the member able to volunteer for a specialist military dog course. Future dog handlers must undergo a fourteen-day review pre-selection which includes training in the feeding, care and basic training of a dog. In addition, they undergo 24 hours of sleep deprivation and intense physical activity while being reviewed by the army's psychological service for their physical and mental resilience. A final test on the knowledge acquired completes this selection process and participation in a military dog-training course is discussed.

Austria has a long record of using dogs in the military. An article in a newspaper dated 25 November 1887 stated: 'For some time past the Austrian troops in Bosnia have been using large dogs for military purposes. The animals are doing such good work that the war Minister has resolved to make a trial with them on a larger scale. During the winter a number of dogs will be trained in patrol and outpost duty, so as to be able to take part in the autumn manoeuvres next year.'

During World War I Austria was part of the Austro-Hungarian Empire and used war dogs for haulage duties in mountainous terrain. At the beginning of World War II war dogs were amalgamated into the German Army after Germany annexed Austria.

With the end of the Cold War, the Austrian military have increasingly assisted border police in controlling the influx of illegal immigrants through Austrian borders. MWDs have been used extensively to assist in this area. Today, MWDs are used for the security of critical radar sites, ammunition stocks and during border operations. During the years under Communist regimes in Eastern Europe, Austrian army dogs would apprehend people along the border between Hungary and Czechoslovakia. While nine out of ten people would give up when confronted by these MWDs, occasionally the dogs were called upon to defend their handlers from those intent on crossing the border.

Austria is unique in that a large percentage of their service dogs are Rottweilers. The Austrian forces believe that the Rottweiler possesses attributes suitable to their needs such as a calm and self-assured nature, courage, an impressive appearance for deterrence, and it does not bark easily and give away the presence of the squad.

The Military Dog School was initially founded in 1958, finally establishing itself in 1964. The Austrian army started with four German shepherds from the Austrian Border Patrol.

All dogs bred and kept by the Austrian army are tested by rigid medical examinations. Service dogs are raised and pre-trained until 20 months at the Milhusta base and are then trained with their future handler for three months. Dog live from then on at their handler's residence until they retire at between eight and nine years of age. They then become the handler's property; no retired dogs are put down.

In Austria, due to the required skills and performance parameters, and in coordination with the military potential canine husbandry and rearing conditions, the following breeds are particularly suitable for training as a military dog. The Rottweiler is bred inhouse primarily as a protection dog. The German shepherd is the most widely used breed in the world and is considered an all-rounder; it is proven for its versatility and as an excellent search dog. Austrian German shepherds are dual-trained depending on their suitability as either rescue dogs or mine detection dogs (MDDs). Belgian malinois' performance characteristics are similar to those of the German shepherd. Through their uncompromising and strong character they are valued mainly for special operations. They can also be trained as explosives sniffer dogs. The labrador retrievers are mainly used for search tasks of any kind (scouts, MDDs, rescue).

Training

The Military Dog Centre in Kaisersteinbruch is the main breeding and training centre for service dogs in the Austrian army. Overall, the army has about 250 military dogs. Domestically, specialist dogs are used on military property for drug detection work by MPs.

MWDs commence training at 15 months. The basic course for military dog handlers is of twelve weeks' duration; further training for specialist dogs takes three months. Integration into family association is held in high regard by the Austrian army; MWDs are fully integrated into the family of their handler.

The military dog kennel centre has the responsibility, regardless of the dog's role in military service, for breeding, rearing, purchase, pre-training, sheltering and caring for military dogs.

The kennel master is responsible for his staff, the care, control and maintenance of all kennels in terms of security and functionality as well as necessary veterinary measures and procurement, storage, quality control and preparation of feed.

Deployment

Military dogs in the Austrian army cover many roles: guard dogs, sniffer dogs, rescue dogs, explosive and drug detection dogs. They are deployed in many foreign countries, as well as in increasingly important domestic duties. The aim of any military use of dogs is to increase the efficiency and safety of deployed forces and to minimise the risk for troops at home and abroad.

Currently, military dogs are employed with the ground forces (army patrol) the Operations Support Command, the Office for Armaments and Defense Technology, the Army Intelligence Office (*Heeresnachrichtenamt*), the Special Operations Forces command and the Foreign Contingents Deployment Group.

Dogs are used to ensure the highest level of security in areas such as technical installations, airports, restricted areas and ammunition dumps. In addition, sniffer dogs are used in the detection of explosives and narcotics. They are deployed in the UN troop contingent in the separation zone between Syria and Israel, and in the Balkans.

Some of the ways MWDs are employed in Austria are in handler protection and the security of any troops at home and abroad. Handler protection is the classic main purpose for military dogs, even in the army. This includes requirements for the protection of objects, roads and people.

Military dogs are particularly suitable for use in intermediate and convergence lines, such as checkpoints and observation posts. They primarily provide detection at night.

Fixed checkpoints and temporary checkpoints both serve to monitor the movement of people and vehicles, especially in regard to contraband, explosives, weapons and ammunition and hidden people. Such control tasks are better conducted with the assistance of dogs.

The use of military dogs in the Special Forces Command is primarily for personal security and explosives detection. Specially trained dogs can thereby contribute significantly to the success of an operation. Dogs used for special operations are robust, have strong nerves and teamwork skills and are able to operate in adverse conditions like darkness or deployment by parachute.

Search and Rescue

Search and rescue operations are always about finding people, whether it is after natural disasters or accidents, or finding missing persons. These operations fall within the framework of AFDRU (Austrian Forces Disaster Relief Unit). Avalanche search is a highly skilled rescue form; both handlers and dogs must be fit and well versed in survival principals themselves. The unforgiving conditions can at times be as dangerous to the rescuers as they are to the victims.

SWITZERLAND

The Swiss armed forces perform the roles of Switzerland's militia and regular army: under the country's militia system professional soldiers constitute only about 5 per cent of the military personnel. The rest are conscript citizens aged from 20 to 34 years. Because of a long history of neutrality, the army does not take part in armed conflicts, but is part of some peacekeeping missions around the world.

The Military Police

The Military Police (MP) consists of professionals and members of the militia. Their duties include security and protection of the Swiss army. The operational elements of the MP are referred to as 'elements of the first hour', which means after a short preparation these troops can be deployed at home or abroad operationally. They can independently be used by the army or secondarily at the request of civilian authorities. They do not compete with other police agents.

The MP is responsible for:
• security, forensic and traffic duties within the armed forces at home or abroad
• assessment of the military security situation
• espionage and sabotage protection
• protection of the Federal State of Switzerland
• assistance to other authorities in subsidiary security tasks
• explosive ordnance disposal (KAMIR).
• neutralisation of unconventional explosive and incendiary devices
• humanitarian and military demining

The MP use MWDs in the last three roles, as well as in the general security role and narcotic detection role.

The Army Veterinary Service

The Centre for Army Veterinary Service of Animals is located at Schönbühl and provides the training and veterinary care for animals used by the Swiss armed forces. This includes both horses and military working dogs. It has a secondary mission to support civilian agencies in response to spontaneous disaster relief.

The centre is the prospective recruit's first attachment for training in veterinary service, blacksmithing and for the care of dogs. It serves to determine the suitability of a potential military recruit.

The organisation has a separate military school for students of veterinary medicine (lieutenant, veterinary doctor), which provides some of the best training in Switzerland.

The Veterinary Service of the Armed Forces, the *Kompetenzzentrum*, is also responsible for the procurement and training of the army MWDs.

The Swiss militia system stipulates that soldiers keep their own personal equipment, including all personal weapons, at home. This is also true for an

MWD handler. After completing a recruit MWD course, the welfare of the dog has to be ensured by the handler, who is responsible for the dog's operational status and fitness at home.

Experts of the Veterinary Service of the Armed Forces can check on a handler's status at any time. This is achieved by regular weekly continuation training sessions, and at least one annual test with the service dog is undertaken by regular instructors. All training guidelines are set out by the training school.

Many of the militia MWDs are used in the search and rescue role and regularly train for disaster relief missions. Search and rescue (SAR) is an operation with the basic aim of recovering distressed personnel. SAR operations can be, and usually are, conducted in adverse weather conditions and in difficult terrain or environments. It is a natural tendency for injured people to seek a hiding place to protect themselves from further injury or further physiological harm. These hiding places are often overlooked by search parties, and medics can be aided by the use of SAR dogs.

SAR dogs complement peacetime humanitarian aid missions in locating casualties of natural disasters such as avalanche, flooding or earthquakes. This is also a method of projecting a positive image for the defence force helping the civilian community.

THE NETHERLANDS

In October 2002 a tri-nation detachment of eighteen Dutch, Danish and Norwegian F-16 ground attack aircraft and one Dutch KDC-10 tanker deployed to Manas Air Base in Kyrgyzstan in support of ground forces in Afghanistan as part of Operation Enduring Freedom. The Royal Netherlands Air Force (RNLAF) returned to Manas Air Base in September 2004 with five F-16s and one KDC-10 in support of the presidential elections of Afghanistan. This time the aircraft flew under the NATO ISAF flag. As part of this detachment the security element was made up of an undisclosed number of MWDs from the RNLAF. Their role has expanded to include base security protection, active patrolling with ISAF forces and the operation of EDD teams in the Uruzgan province.

Dutch RNLAF MWD teams in situ use Bushmaster armoured vehicles. These vehicles are Australian-designed and the NetherlandsgGovernment purchased several versions after close cooperation working with Australian troops in Afghanistan. RNLAF dog handlers operate within the confines of the base conducting searches and conduct regular patrols via foot, vehicles and helicopter outside the base too. Dutch MWDs in Afghanistan included EDDs, MDDs and general patrol dogs.

Dutch Gendarmie

The Royal Netherlands Marechaussee (in Dutch *Koninklijke Marechaussee*, abbreviated to *Kilometresar*) is one of the four services of the armed forces of the Netherlands. It is a gendarmerie force performing Military Police (MP) and civil police duties. The main tasks for the Marechaussee are border protection, MP and guard duties. Specialist detection dog teams are used in the protection of borders and police dogs are used in both military and civilian police roles.

FORMER SOVIET UNION COUNTRIES

RUSSIA

It is generally known that dogs were used to attack and repel enemies on a battlefield in ancient times before firearms were invented. To this end, large physically vigorous dogs were bred. With the invention of firearms and their further developments in destruction ranges and firing speeds, fight dogs lost their significance on a battlefield.

The Russian army began to use dogs as fortress sentries who warned the guards of an approaching enemy and accompanied army troops during their campaigns. Dogs also performed communication jobs, carried ammunition and delivered first aid.

In Western armies working dogs became widely used before World War I. There were no more than 300 dogs in the Russian army during World War I; the Russian army command did not give due attention to the use of dogs. Russian sanitary dogs were trained to search for the wounded and guide rescuers to them. Up until the Russian Revolution the Russian army used many hundreds of dogs in roles similar to other countries such as messenger, trench guard and in the rescue role. The Red Army leadership then took a practical step to develop military dog breeding and in 1924 set up the Central Kennel in Moscow to train military and sporting dogs.

Central School of Military Working Dog Training: 1924

On 23 August 1924 the Revolutionary Military Council of the Red Army issued an order (Order No 1089) to establish the Central Experimental Military and Sporting Dog Kennel in Moscow (Kuskovo).

Order 1089 states: 'Experimental kennels for military and sports dogs are to be set up in the Red Army units in order to conduct experiments on the use of dogs for military purposes. To that end:

1. The Combat Training Directorate of the Red Army is to set up the Central Experimental Military and Sporting Dogs Kennel/School under the *Vystrel* [shot] Higher Small Arms Firing and Tactical School in Moscow in order to train dogs for scouting, communication, sentry, delivering first aid and assisting defence depot guards.

2. The announced staff and provisions on both the Central and district military and sporting dog kennels/schools are to be put into effect.

3. Work on establishment of the Central Kennel/School is to start immediately and should be finished by 1 November this year when school is to commence. A special order will be issued on timing of establishment of district kennels/schools.

4. On completion of theoretical and practical dog training, the Combat Training Directorate of the Red Army and the command of districts and armies are to set up special commissions in order to assess the dogs' level of training and the advisability of further training.'

The Order is signed by Iosif Unshlikht, Deputy Chair of the Revolutionary Military Council, on 23 August 1924.

Colonel Nikita Evtushenko, whose military occupation was communications, became the first head of the Military and Sporting Dog School. He accepted his appointment with interest, though he was not familiar with his new occupation. However, even before this appointment he had been involved in dog training as the first head of the Central Section for Working Dog Training under the Hunters Union, and later under the OSOAVIAKHIM (Union of Societies of Assistance to Defence and Aviation-Chemical Construction of the USSR). Back then there were already societies of hunters and anglers in the Red Army units. Military hunters, who already had experience with hunting dogs, became the school's first attendees. Colonel Evtushenko's initiative and administrative skills sped establishment and development of military dog training in the army.

1934

As suggested by the Air Force Research Institute, the school started experimental work on the possibility of air dropping dogs behind enemy lines and using them for target demolition. This job for dogs was called an airborne service (during World War II, it was called diversionary service). Training covered three aspects: rail demolition, railway and highway bridge demolition and oil tank demolition.

In order to train the staff and dogs, a parachute tower and a 100-metre railway was constructed at the unit training site. June and October 1934 saw tests for airborne dogs at the Monino airfield in the Moscow Region. Training of airborne dogs did not cause any difficulties due to available experience with anti-tank dog training. With the airborne dog service, the focus was on training personnel who would be able to define a tactically correct target and choose the right moment to release a dog. Such operations were to be preceded by proper reconnaissance of designated objectives.

During the Great Patriotic War (1941-1945), the Central School did not carry out any special airborne or diversionary dog training for combat operations. However, it was Subcolonel Alexander Mazover's personal initiative to use a dog from his Mine Detection Dog Unit No.37 to demolish a railway on the Belorussian front in 1943.

On 19 August, not far from Polotsk, Private First Class Filatov from Senior Sergeant Bychkov's group released a dog called Dina. The dog covered the distance between the hideout to the railway, dropped a special separable pack on the railway and quickly returned to its handler. Fifteen to eighteen seconds later, an explosion destroyed the railway bed and wrecked a troop train since the dog had been re-released towards the approaching train.

1941-1945

The Central School's active participation in the operations of the Soviet Forces during the Great Patriotic War (1941-1945) yielded the following outcomes:

1. 168 units and subunits were formed, ranging from separate platoon and companies to special separate regiments:
   - 2 special regiments
   - 21 separate battalions
   - 45 separate detachments
   - 100 separate platoons and companies

2. Special services:
   - 13 anti-tank dog battalions (detachments)
   - 18 mine-detection dog battalions
   - 36 sledge dog battalions
   - 4 messenger dog detachment
   - 2 special regiments
   - 69 separate sled teams

In order to staff all the units, the School trained:
   - 3,000 officers
   - 8,000 sergeants
   - 32,000 handlers
   Total: 43,000 personnel

The army was supplied with 68,000 dogs from different regions of the country through dog training clubs and individuals. The Central School alone received 20,000 dogs. 10,000 dogs came from Moscow and Moscow Region, 5,500 from Sverdlovsk, 2,500 from Kiev, 1,334 from Kalinin and 1,124 from Kazan. Individual dog fanciers and even schoolchildren specially raised dogs and then handed them over to the army. Those dog fanciers who gave their dogs to the school gained the right to get a puppy from the school's breed kennel at no cost after the war. The kennel gave 1,200 puppies of working and hunting dogs to clubs and individuals.

Soviets tested anti-tank (AT) dogs during the military conflict with Japan in 1939, destroying several Japanese light tanks. In August 1941 Soviets had ten army units of AT dogs (consisting of four companies until July 1942, later of two companies; each company had 126 dogs). Each AT dog unit also had a rifle platoon with snipers for killing the missed dogs with explosives. The first action AT dogs saw was during the battle of Moscow in autumn 1941; the 28th Unit of AT dogs destroyed 42 German tanks and two armoured cars during the Battle of Stalingrad. In one battle fifteen of seventeen dogs managed to reach the German tanks.

In 1943 (when AT dog units were disbanded) the Soviet Army had two regiments of AT dogs and 168 separate units of AT dogs. Taking into consideration such large number of AT dog units, only 300 German tanks are reported to have been destroyed. That means that every unit with 100-odd dogs could destroy only two tanks on average: a very ineffective ratio.

AT dogs were employed in the biggest battles: before Moscow, before Stalingrad and at Kursk. The dogs destroyed a sufficient number of tanks for the survivors to be considered worthy of the honour of taking part in the victory parade in the Red Square.

Messenger dogs delivered 200,000 messages; doves delivered 3,745 telegrams; and communication dogs pulled 7,883 kilometres (4,898 miles) of telephone cable (specially equipped sled teams were effectively used to reel out cables).

The Red Army's dogs had respected military trades, such as *razvedka*, searching for wounded on the battlefield. During the whole war, casualty and ambulance sled teams (4,500 teams trained, with 43 per cent of the school's dogs used for this purpose) evacuated 500,000 soldiers and officers and their arms from the battlefields, and transported 3,682 tonnes of different loads.

Mine detection dogs (MDDs), who made up 28 per cent of dog force, detected and deactivated 4 million mines and explosive devices; checked 1,223 square kilometres (759 square miles) for mines; detected 394 minefields; checked 15,000 kilometres (9,320 miles) of roads; detected 193 minefields at home; cleared 52 lanes in the minefields; cleared 3,973 bridges, storage depots and buildings; and cleared 33 major cities in the USSR and Europe of mines (including Minsk, Kharkov, Kiev, Odessa, Lvov, Warsaw, Vienna, Dresden, Berlin, Budapest and Belgrade). Sentry dogs raised 296 alerts.

1960–1965

In 1960, under the direction of the Defence Ministry responding to the request of the All-Russia Association of the Blind, a guide dog training school was set up in the grounds of the Central School. Nikolai Orekhov was a longstanding head of this school. In 1965 the Guide Dog School moved to the town of Kupavna in the Moscow region.

The Shah of Afghanistan requested the Soviet government provide assistance in establishing a dog training school in the Afghan army. On 21 January, the Central School sent a group of its personnel and ten German shepherds, led by Major Viktor Presnov, to Kabul. The school in the Afghan army was set up. In 1963 Major Presnov's group returned to the Central School, bringing Afghan hounds and Central Asian shepherds for the Central School's breed kennel.

1980–1988

In this period the school was training mine detection, guard and tracking specialists to perform combat missions in the Republic of Afghanistan. The school's graduates performed the most challenging and dangerous mine-clearing tasks, displaying courage and heroism. One out of every three handerls was awarded a medal. Together with their faithful MDDs, they covered endless kilometres of mountain roads and paths. There are many examples of dogs locating up to 100 elaborately laid mines.

From 1980 to 1988, 610 dogs were trained, including 408 MDDs, 177 guard dogs and 25 dogs to detect explosives in transport. The MDDs located more than 7,000 mines.

Soviet combat engineers used dogs to sniff for landmines during their war in Afghanistan. German shepherds were the breed of choice. The Afghans tried a number of ways to baffle the Soviet Union's dogs, like wrapping the mines in cellophane or sprinkling them with motor oil. Neither method was very successful. Dogs are still used today to help locate the thousands of landmines left in Afghanistan; these MDDs are used by local forces trained and sponsored by the United Nations or civilian aid agencies.

There is plenty of evidence that *Spetsnaz* (Russian Special Forces) used MWDs in Afghanistan to carry out their traditional tasks: protecting groups from surprise attack, seeking out the enemy, detecting mines, and helping in the interrogation of captured Afghan resistance fighters. They are just as mobile as the men themselves, since they can be dropped by parachute in special soft containers. The engineer reconnaissance units train MDDs in all weather conditions.

MDDs have proved very valuable to the Soviet/Russian forces over the years. They were used extensively in Afghanistan and more recently in the Chechen War.

1988–Present
Today the centre trains sentry, mine detection, tracking and search and rescue dogs. The centre's graduate handlers, together with their dogs, demonstrated complete professionalism when fulfilling combat tasks to restore constitutional order and eliminate armed gangs and terrorist camps in the Chechen Republic. Professionalism of military dog specialists was highly appreciated during the peacekeeping operations in South Ossetia, Abkhazia and Tajikistan.

From 2005 to 2009, the centre trained 2,784 dogs, including 221 MDDs, 2,431 sentry dogs 93 tracking dogs and 39 search and rescue dogs.

The most frightening, demoralising opponent of the *Spetsnaz* soldier has always been and always will be the dog. No electronic devices and no enemy firepower has such an effect on his morale as the appearance of dogs. The enemy's dogs always appear at the most awkward moment, when a group exhausted by a long trek is enjoying a brief uneasy sleep, when their legs are totally worn out and their ammunition is used up. Surveys conducted among soldiers, sergeants and officers in *Spetsnaz* produce the same answer again and again: the last thing they want to come up against is the enemy's dogs.

The heads of the GRU (Russian foreign military intelligence) have conducted far-reaching studies into this question and come to the conclusion that the best way to deal with dogs is to use dogs as well.

Just as the Russians previously trained anti-tank dogs in World War II for suicide missions, the Soviet doctrine in any modern European war called on the use of dogs to carry out similar missions and destroy the enemy's nuclear weapons sites.

It is a great deal easier to teach a dog to get up to a missile or an aircraft unnoticed than it is to get it to go under a roaring, thundering tank. As before, the dog would carry a charge weighing about 4 kilograms (9 pounds), but charges of that weight are today much more powerful than they were in World War II and the detonators are incomparably more sophisticated and foolproof. Detonators have been developed that detonate only on contact with metal but do not go off on accidental contact with long grass, branches or other objects. The intelligent dog, with proper training, quickly becomes capable seeking out, correctly identifying and attacking important targets. Such targets include complicated electronic equipment, aerials, missiles, aircraft, staff cars, cars carrying VIPs and occasionally individuals. All of this makes the *Spetsnaz* dog a frightening and dangerous enemy.

Apart from everything else, the presence of dogs with a *Spetsnaz* group appreciably raises the morale of the officers and the men. Some especially powerful and vicious dogs are trained for one purpose alone—to guard the group and to destroy the enemy's dogs if they appear.

para-military

Today there are many units within Russia that operate dogs in the para-military role, including border guard units and special police units. The Soviet KGB border guards use tracker dogs on the mountainous terrain bordering the Soviet Union and Afghanistan. Entry into the KGB border guards canine unit was highly selective; a recruit had to have an unimpeachable political background. Entry was normally limited to applicants of Russian, Byelorussian or Ukrainian descent.

LATVIA

The decision to form a subunit of military dog handlers was made in 2004. The first military dogs and dog handlers in the Latvian National Armed Forces have been trained for detection of improvised explosive devices. Training was organised in close cooperation with the state police.

Today, training of the dogs and handlers of the Latvian National Armed Forces takes part in the training centre of the State Border Guard, where dog handlers can acquire and improve their professional skills.

The tasks of Latvian military dogs include the detection of possible improvised explosive devices (IEDs) during visits by Latvian and foreign state officials. The Latvian Military Police (MP) currently have ten service dogs, who operate in support of Provost Operations. The dogs are typically trained to search, track, defend their handler and attack when necessary.

Even though a para-military organisation, Latvia's border guard unit operates MWDs in security and patrol roles in Afghanistan. In 2009 three Latvian dog handlers took part in EULEX (European Union Rule of Law Mission) in Kosovo. In 2010 one dog handler and one service dog were still in Kosovo.

The history of Latvian border guard dog handling is very short. The Latvians began to use service dogs in 1994 (Latvian border guards were only established in 1991) after Russian withdrawal. Before World War II border guard units did not have service dogs, and from then until Latvian independence, the Soviets looked after border security. The first dog handlers were trained at the Soviet dog-handlers school.

The first dogs used in border guard service were at Liepaja, Daugavpils and in the border guard training centre in Rezekne. Today this establishment has around 140 service dogs, making it the biggest dog-handler service in Latvia. Other services that use dogs in Latvia are customs (25), police (20) and prisons (15).

The largest number of dogs are located on the Eastern border (with Russia and Belorussia) where trained dogs are used for tracking, patrolling, searching for humans, drugs search and explosive search.

Latvia participates in international operations organised by the European Union Agency (FRONTEX), resulting in the apprehension of many illegal migrants from Pakistan and Afghanistan.

Since 1997 Latvia has organised an international competition for dog handlers every year. The competition alternates between tracking dogs and drug-detection dogs each year. Since 2006, the international dog biathlon has involved the military, border guards, police, customs, prison services and guests from Lithuania, Estonia, Finland, Byelorussia, Poland and Moldova.

The dog training school is responsible for the planning, organisation and management of dog handler activities. This includes the training of specialist dog handlers and general service dogs, and the breeding of service dogs. It also carries out scientific research work in the field of dog breeding, dog handler activities and experience analysis.

Approximately 85 service dogs are used during patrols on the green border, conducting terrain search with an average of five service dogs at one border guarding station. Twenty-seven drug detection dogs are used for vehicle, railway transport and luggage examination. They are situated at road, railway, seaport and airport border control points. Approximately seven explosive service dogs are used for vehicle and luggage examination checks, as well as providing security measures in cooperation with other law enforcement institutions. The major breed of dogs used by all services is the German shepherd.

LITHUANIA

Lithuania's defence system is based on the concept of 'total and unconditional defence'. The goal of Lithuania's defence policy is to integrate the country into Western security and defence structures. The defence department is responsible for combat forces, search and rescue and intelligence operations.

A newly established canine section of the Prevention and Pre-trial Investigation Board of the Military Police operates in the Lithuanian armed forces. As it is a young institution, it is still developing. Currently the section employs a small number of military personnel and a few dogs. The canine section is tasked with the prevention of criminal acts and other law violations. Military dogs are trained to search for narcotic substances, explosion devices and weapons, guard service facilities, carry out search and rescue work, to suppress riots and to track.

The Lithuanian Military Police have established very high standards for their MWDs, and in addition to the above specialist roles dogs are also employed in defending persons or objects under guard against attack, conducting convoy escorts, detaining individuals escaping from custody or detaining a person suspected of committing a criminal act, outrage against public order or breach of disciplinary order in a military territory.

Among other institutions that use dogs for carrying out assigned tasks are the State Border Guard Service Internal Regiments and the VIP Protection Department, all operating under the Ministry of the Interior of the Republic of Lithuania. There are 5,400 border guards charged with controlling and maintaining the Lithuanian border.

In Afghanistan, Lithuanian Special Operations Force (SOF) units have participated in a number of missions. There is believed to be a SOF military dog handler in Afghanistan. It is believed that the MWD was obtained in situ.

Lithuanian messenger dogs were used during World War II. Other roles included guard and patrol duty in Axis army units manned by Lithuanians. The Lithuanians were trained by the Third Reich during World War II and at the end of the war many of these dogs were taken over by the Russians.

EASTERN EUROPE

Since the decline of the Soviet Union many Eastern European countries have emerged into new nations or split into states based on ethnic lines that existed before World War II. Many have retained the Soviet system of using military working dogs (MWDs) primarily in the guard role. Some have adapted MWDs to roles suitable to their new status within the European Union, undertaking peacekeeping missions by using dogs such as explosive detection dogs (EDDs). For some of the less wealthy Eastern Bloc countries, where a new, struggling economy is developing, MWDs are seen as an economic low-tech force protection asset to guard deactivated military bases or sensitive material storage sites left by the former Soviet regime.

Dogs are often used by para-military border guard units; where once they may have kept people in, they now protect their nation's borders by conducting drug and illegal alien patrol missions.

ESTONIA

Since 2006 approximately 120 Estonian soldiers have been participating in missions in Afghanistan. The majority of the Estonian units are stationed in the Helmand province, Southern Afghanistan as a part of the UK Helmand Task Force. The Estonian infantry company in Helmand participates in combat operations against anti-government armed groups, in particular the Taliban, alongside British and Afghan units.

The explosive ordnance disposal team of the Rescue Board, with bomb-sniffing dogs, participated in the anti-terrorism operation Enduring Freedom from July 2002 until June 2005. Their responsibility, as part of an international brigade, was to clear the area around Kabul of leftover explosives. Their last operation took place at the beginning of 2005, when a team of five with two bomb detection dogs served in Bagram Airbase near Kabul.

BELARUS

The military of the armed forces of Belarus defend the interests of the Belarusian state. This task, however, is complex, because of various agreements that have been signed with Russia. Membership in the Commonwealth of Independent States, as well as the 1996 treaty on the Union of Russia and Belarus, and the Treaty of the Formation of a Union State in 1999, have all confirmed a close partnership with Russia. Belarus maintains a large number of dogs in the Border Protection Service as well as the military.

The national Dog Training Centre in Minsk is one of the best in Europe, offering dedicated service in training dogs for a variety of uses. It is a large, spacious complex with more than 100 MWDs being trained at one time. Every dog is assigned a dedicated handler from the start. They are not separated, even after the dog transfers to its operational task.

HUNGARY

The main task of the Hungarian defence forces (HDF) is to defend the sovereignty and territorial integrity of the Republic of Hungary and to contribute to the collective defence of NATO on the basis of the North Atlantic Treaty. The Hungarian defence forces are also ready to participate in peace support and humanitarian actions governed under the auspices of the United Nations and other international organisations.

History

Asymmetric warfare and force protection require the introduction of new combat techniques as well as development in technology, armaments and methodology. For this reason the HDF decided to set up a special, dog-assisted explosive ordnance demolition (EOD) subunit within the structure of the EOD Battalion. The development of this new HDF capability started in late 2005.

Selection and Training

Choosing the right dog for this unusual job is a very important part of the Hungarian defence forces' work. A proper explosive detection dog (EDD) has an open, friendly, confident character, and a well-built, athletic and healthy body. Before the forces purchase a new dog it must go through a strict veterinary check and suitability test, where their abilities are checked. This will ensure that they will be able to carry out their duties for a long time.

The Hungarian defence forces usually buy dogs between the age of six and eighteen months. Principally they work with German shepherds but other breeds are also encountered (for example, malinois, labrador retriever, Australian kelpie and border collie). After the selection process, sniffer dogs and handlers begin their training in the Police Dog Training Centre according to a cooperation agreement between the two responsible ministries.

The basic training consists of obedience, dexterity and special explosive-detecting instruction. This basic course takes five months. During EDD training, Hungarian defence forces dogs become able to recognise many types of normal and mixed explosive smells in real-life conditions.

Present Day Operations

In the beginning of 2007, EDDs were deployed to the Hungarian-led Provincial Reconstruction Team (Hun PRT) in the north of Afghanistan. Since then, they have served as an essential part of this mission, searching for explosives and ensuring the safety of various buildings, and airports.

SLOVENIA

Dogs in the Slovenian armed forces first appeared in 1991 during Slovenia's war of independence. At that time, some members of the then territorial defence force led the call for the use of military dogs. The dogs were normally used to protect important buildings, warehouses and transport points as guards. At the official end of the Revolutionary War, the 1st Special Brigade was set up for training dogs and guides. The Military Police (MP) cooperate with civil police dog units in Slovenia, and with various dog sections in other European armies.

In 1998 the unit for the breeding and training of military dogs (EVŠVP) was placed under veterinary service. The unit deals with the schooling of dogs and handlers for the various specialty needs of the whole service. The unit is located in the south of Slovenia near the Kočevski River. In 2005 a new centre was built with a capacity for 50 dogs. Within the canine centre is a modern veterinary clinic responsible for the health of all service dogs and tasked with breeding service dogs.

The Military Medical unit is attached to the Support Command and carries out activities and measures to provide medical care, as well as to achieve, maintain and protect the optimal health of the Slovenian armed forces service members. Within this structure is the Veterinary Unit, which carries out preventive measures regarding contagious and parasitic diseases, and monitors epizoology around the world. It systematically breeds dogs for the purposes of the Slovenian Armed Forces, and trains them in detecting explosives and illegal drugs, searching for missing persons and performing guard-patrol tasks. The unit also trains all dog-handlers of the Slovenian armed forces.

The unit breeds an indigenous dog: the karst shepherd, which has been around since 1641. These dogs have been used for centuries by farmers to ward off wolves from their flocks.

Today the dog training centre conducts training for specialist search and general police dogs for the needs of the MP. Units with dogs and handlers have been in Afghanistan continuously for the past five years in the Herat province.

Since 1994, the Slovenian armed forces 17th Military Police Battalion has had several service dogs. Their function is to perform MP working dog duties, namely crowd control, tracking and attacking. Their mission upon establishment was inherited from the former territorial defense force in 1991. By 1994 the first group completed training MWDs for general use. In 1999 they started to use dogs to assist police in Postojna.

In that same year the first military dogs were trained to search for illicit drugs. In 2002 the unit received the first dogs trained to detect explosives. The first Slovenian armed forces service dog used for the illegal search of drugs was deployed as part of ISAF in Afghanistan in response to the fifth Slovenian contingent request in 2006. They remain in Afghanistan on that same mission today.

The 17th Military Police Battalion uses nine dogs, comprising eight Belgian malinois and a labrador. Three are for general duties, three for the detection of mines and resources, and three for the detection of illicit drugs. They are all housed in barracks at Franc Rozman Stane in Ljubljana.

The dogs used as general patrol MP dogs must be well socialised very as they must work around the general public as well as on military operations. Dogs for general use, or defense dogs are used to control law and order at various events, to intervene in cases of breaches in military areas, to protect facilities and to apprehend military or civilian personnel in military zones. They also assist in the arrest, transfer and monitoring of persons who have committed offences.

Dogs for specialised uses are selected for their instincts. They are well socialised and are capable of searching in different conditions and terrains and in the presence of various distractions, including people.

MDDs are trained to detect explosive devices on vehicles and vessels at various facilities and anywhere where terrorist activity is possible. They are trained in the identification of several types of explosives, which they indicate by sitting passively. Narcotics detection dogs (NDDs) are trained to recognise five basic substances: marijuana, hashish, amphetamines, heroin and cocaine. They detect with an active response, such as scratching, barking or biting at the location of the hidden drug.

Poland

Poland started using MWDs after World War I when they regained independence. At this time the dominant breeds were Airedale terriers, German shepherds and Dobermans. They were used mainly as communication dogs or guard dogs, as well as searching for the wounded, delivering first aid to soldiers and ammunition carriage. A military communication manual described all matters concerning training and using military working dogs for messenger work.

In 1937 the commander of the Communication Forces gave an order introducing about 400 dogs into the Communication Forces. That year is now recognised as the official introduction of dogs into the Polish army. Dogs were used to carry food and forward ammunition using special trolleys. Sanitary dogs carried medications to the front line, and searched for wounded soldiers and those missing in action. They were used as a guard dogs as well. Until 1934, 24 dogs served with Polish soldiers on Westerplatte.

After World War II the Polish armed forces mainly used patrol, guard and search dogs. A Military Dog Training Centre in Pulawy was situated within the Military Veterinary Research Institute led by Veterinary Corps from 1955.

In 2003 this centre was moved to Celestynów, with new training facilities located in a friendlier forest environment. In 2007 the military introduced explosive and weapon detection, as well as drug-searching courses for handlers and dogs who were working periodically (on a six-month rotation in Afghanistan).

Czech Republic

Military working dogs, known there as service dogs, are primarily used by the Army of the Czech Republic (ACR) for guard and patrol work. Furthermore, dogs are trained in specialty work: to find drugs, explosives and weapons, or search and rescue. The professional army has a total of 1,350 service dogs, which are assigned to a total of 82 departments. The Army uses German shepherds, Belgian malinois, briards, Rottweilers, Dobermans, giant schnauzers and a few individuals of other breeds.

The ACR believes the dog is the second oldest weapon system used in the armed forces, after the offensive blade. The dog has characteristics that have not yet been surpassed by technology. Even the most expensive electronic security systems are not perfect. Systems only draw attention to the disruption of the object or entry of unauthorised persons into the guarded area. No technology-based equipment is capable of locating and apprehending intruders, as dogs are.

ACR service dogs are used in guarding, especially in combination with electronic alarm systems and surveillance, at ammunition depots and military camps and in the protection of high value equipment and air bases. Without the dogs, the ACR would be unable to invest in the modern surveillance systems necessary to secure facilities.

The 192nd Military Police (MP) performs the tasks of policing the armed forces, and are staffed only by professional soldiers, not conscripts. The MP is headed by the Chief of Military Police, who reports directly to the Minister of Defence. The MP was established on 21 January 1991. It enforces the prevention of misuse of drugs, protection of weapons, ammunition and explosives, as well as crime prevention generally.

The MP sets out conditions for the use of dogs, including the fact that MP MWDs are required to use a muzzle, except under certain conditions. The MP operates specialist drug-search dogs, which are used mainly to control illegal use by conscripts.

The ACR rapid deployment brigade has trained parachute and helicopter-borne MWD teams. These teams are inserted in rugged terrain in order to conduct forward reconnaissance against ambushes. This unit also deploys MWDs on overseas missions.

Guard dogs are divided into the following tasks: guarding facilities with a handler; patrolling off-leash (fenced-in area); fixed on a swing chain (on block); and guarding in pairs. Dogs in lone positions are checked every four hours. The dog may, under normal climatic conditions, be on duty for a maximum of twelve hours.

Patrol dogs are divided into the following tasks: patrol dog defence (basic guard dog) and patrol dog versatile (police dog).

There are also categories of search/tracker dogs, who are required to track a scent up to five hours old for eight kilometres long a scent trail.

Specialist Dogs

In the past the ACR has used dogs trained in mine-detection and to carry ammunition. Search dogs and drugs-, explosives- and weapons-detection dogs are mainly assigned to the MP.

The dog school trains approximately 600 people and 450 dogs yearly. In recent years the ACR has used hundreds of handlers and dogs for tasks in difficult climatic conditions in the Gulf War, Bosnia, Kosovo, in the separation zone in Cyprus and in various military missions in the Middle East, among others. Even in peacetime, European countries require greater use of internal security forces, such as MWD teams, in the fight against ever-increasing crime and terrorism.

CROATIA

The fundamental role and purpose of the Croatian Army is to protect vital national interests of the Republic of Croatia and defend the sovereignty and territorial integrity of the state. As part of this mission Croatia supplies troops to aid NATO and ISAF missions, including MWD teams, and helps train friendly forces.

Croatia currently has no troops with the US-led forces in Iraq. However, one of the activities through which the country contributes to building stability in the Republic of Iraq is carried out by the Training Centre for Military Dog Handlers. Six members of Iraqi security forces and their leader have been trained as handlers with EDDs. This course lasted seven months and was carried out with Croatian dogs raised at the breeding section of the Training Centre. The Croatian donation is an unprecedented gesture to the violence-ridden country and the dogs were handed over by ministry officials in a ceremony at Baghdad airport.

The training of Iraqi security forces was carried out as part of the NATO Training Implementation mission—Iraq (NMTI). Recently the Croatian press reported that Iraq requires 600 more dogs trained in detecting landmines or IEDs, and it is reported that Croatia leads the list of preferred trainers, over US and South African interests.

The MWD program, which includes breeding and training military and official dogs, is conducted in the Training Centre in Dugo Selo. The training centre has existed since 1992 as a part of the Armed Forces of the Republic of Croatia. The training centre also provides training for official dogs of the Ministry of Justice and Ministry of Interior. Depending on their character, dogs are trained for guarding, protection, or detection of drugs and explosives. The trained dogs are used by several units of the Croatian Army, especially in peacekeeping missions, for the detection of drugs and explosives.

The working life of these trained dogs is up to eight years, after which they are retired and usually settled by their guides.

High NATO Training Standards

MWDs are Croatia's elite four-legged soldiers. At the training school for dogs and handlers, young German shepherds and Belgian malinois, Rottweilers and labradors will spend six months learning how to find hidden drugs or explosives, bring down a runaway suspect while keeping their cool under fire, and never disobeying their handlers. Many of them may soon replace the MWD already in situ at the NATO-led peacekeeping mission in Afghanistan. Croatian MP and dogs have served there for the past three years.

Superb training is vital if MWDs are to make it in the real world, and superb training of dogs is what Croatia's army prides itself on, having forged the skills in the 1991-1995 War of Independence.

Croatia has begun to adapt to NATO standards, hoping to join the alliance in the next few years. To that aim, Military Police joined a project, co-financed by the UK and Denmark, where dog trainers from each country compare their experiences.

Croatian MWDs already have a reputation for excellent search techniques and reliability. Croatia hopes to become NATO's regional centre for training military dogs. This would also generate a profit, as a trained dog can fetch between 10,000 and 30,000 Euros.

To retain and promote these high standards Croatia runs several large exercises each year. MWDs attend in explosive detection and general patrol roles. Jackal Stone 09 is an international military exercise that took place in the Josip Jovic barracks in Udbina. Nearly 1,500 participants from ten countries—Albania, Hungary, Lithuania, Macedonia, Poland, Romania, Sweden, Ukraine, the United States and Croatia—participate in the exercise. The organisers of the exercise were the Croatian Armed Forces (CAF) and the technical coordinator was the Special Operations Battalion (BSD). Beside BSD members, all three services of the CAF and members of the Ministry of Interior participate in this exercise, the biggest in Croatia since the nation joined the NATO alliance.

Even though this is a dangerous mission for Croatian MWDs, only one of dozens of dogs trained by Croatia in the last fifteen years has died in action, and this was after his parachute failed to open during a drop. The MWD is buried in a small cemetery at the far end of the barracks of the Dog Training School reserved for Croatian army dogs: the only one of its kind in this part of Europe. Each of a few dozen small tombstones carries the dog's name, age and specialisation.

Military Police

Croatian Military Police in the MP Company (KilometresNB) contribute to NATO assignments and are regarded as having a high degree of capability and professionalism. During important operations in Kabul, Croatian MPs are assigned important positions, including the Military Police Task Force (MPTF), which comprises the national team of military crime police and MWD teams. Every rotation of the MP has MWD handlers. These dogs are used for the detection of drugs or explosives, or protection work. As Croatia is the only country with search dogs in Kabul, the section has a national organisation. It is headed by a member of the CAF who decides how the in-demand dogs are used.

Mediterranean Countries

Greece

The emblem of the Greek Military Guard-Dogs Squads has the following motto from the historian Pindarus: 'When you come face to face with your enemy, you must exterminate him by making use of any means.'

The Hellenic Air Force (HAF) was the pioneer in military working dog (MWD) employment. In 1989 it established ground defence guarding units, training guard dogs along with Non-Commissioned Officers (NCOs) in the protection of its air force bases. To this end, the Guards–Dogs Training Centre (GDTC) was established at Koropi and Attika the same year. In 1990 the Hellenic Army also began to use military dogs for guarding its units.

At first, the Dog Training Centre provided training and veterinary aid for the dogs of the HAF and the Hellenic Army. In 1997 the Hellenic Army organised its own training centres and veterinary clinics at Larissa and Salonica. Today, the dogs of the HAF and the Hellenic Navy (HN), which began to use military dogs only recently, are trained at the Air Force Koropi Centre. Moreover, training courses of six months' duration are provided for new dog trainers and three-month training courses are offered to platoon commanders of the HAF and the HN guard dog squads. A veterinary clinic also operates at the centre, providing medical treatment for the military dogs of the HAF, the Hellenic Army, the HN, the Hellenic Police, the Hellenic Fire-fighting Corps and the Hellenic Harbour Police Corps.

Secret weapon unveiled. This 12-pound Jack Russell terrier, Juul, is no pet. She's one of the navy's military working dogs, attached to the kennel at Naval Station Norfolk. Her size makes it impractical for use as a patrol dog but her sense of smell is so keen she can smell even trace amounts of drugs. *All Hands* magazine photo by JO1 Joseph Gunder.

Tactical use of MWDs in all environments, including land, sea and air, is required of the modern dog handler.

US Army Staff Sgt. Kevin Reese and his military working dog Grek wait at a safe house before conducting an assault against insurgents in Buhriz, Iraq. US Army Soldiers from 5th Battalion, 20th Infantry Regiment, 2nd Infantry Division and Iraqi army soldiers are

going house-to-house in a search for weapons caches and enemy fighters after more than 1,000 residents of this Baqubah suburb were displaced by Al-Qaeda insurgents. US Air Force photo by Staff Sgt. Stacy L. Pearsall.

An Israeli dog handler taking point on a patrol. Infantry commanders understand the value of such an aid and Oketz is always in demand.

This French army dog handler carries not only his standard infantry load, but also water and supplies for his MWD.

An Israeli soldier and dog wearing battlefield equipment.

Perhaps one of the most valuable roles of an MWD is as a force multiplier. In the First Gulf War, thousands of Iraqi POWs were guarded by a single MWD team.

A Greek naval MWD handler during an urban warfare exercise.

Traditionally MWDs have guarded bases at night, often in peacetime as lone sentinels. Photo by Pfc. Rhonda Roth-Cameron, US Army.

Because of quarantine restrictions in the UK, MWDs have to spend six months in Cyprus after every tour of duty. RAF Police dog handlers wore Military Police arm flashes for ease of Coalition force recognition.

Swedish MWD handlers patrol in extreme environmental conditions including Arctic and mountainous terrain.

Austrian special forces join NATO's Operation Cold Response, one of Europe's biggest military exercises, in Narvik, Norway. Dropping from 10,000ft, they glide in order to land unnoticed. The dogs often carry cameras and are trained to attack anyone carrying a weapon.

Some dogs are official mascots and stray mutts that soldiers pick up in battle. Both bring companionship and increase morale among the troops.

This Colombian army dog is trained to find landmines. These detection dogs are from Pedro Nel Ospina Military Base in Bello, Colombia.

Australian Military Police dog handlers attached to the International Stabilisation Force regularly take their canine friends on ANZAC patrols in and around the streets of suburban Dili.

The RAVC is one of the smallest Corps in the British army, yet provides invaluable support to the Army's animals and serves worldwide with them today.

In addition to guarding, the HAF has extended the areas of the military dogs' activities by training guard squads in specialist drugs- and explosives-detection and participating in search and rescue missions.

The breeds used are the German shepherd and the Belgian malinois. These breeds have been selected on the grounds that they satisfactorily combine all the characteristics (strength, stamina, speed, intelligence, strong bite, good sense of smell, balanced behaviour and adaptability to various conditions) required to meet the training demands of the Hellenic forces.

The provision of dogs for the three branches of the Hellenic armed forces came from Germany, which, according to a contract signed with the German army, also guarantees the quality characteristics of the dogs to be supplied and their delivery timetable. At intervals of three to four months, a committee consisting of dog trainers and veterinarians goes to Germany for the selection of dogs, which are then transported to Greece by plane. The selected dogs are evaluated in detail because they must meet the strict criteria set by the Hellenic armed forces. During the last five years the HAF has also accepted dogs (German shepherd and malinois) donated by private owners. Before the donation dogs are accepted they go through an intensive evaluation process.

The dogs' basic training takes 40 days. During this period the teams (guardians and dogs), develop a relationship of mutual trust and cooperation prior to receiving training in basic obedience, encountering invaders, detection through the wind, night patrols, searching buildings and agility exercises. Furthermore, the NCO handlers attend a theory course about the behaviour of dogs, training techniques, patrolling, first aid and veterinary subjects.

After completion of basic training, the teams are assigned to units to undertake operational duties in the ground defence (patrols) role. Almost all HAF units and a great number of army units are posted from the training centre. Depending on the size of their mission or region, between four to 24 dogs are in every unit.

Dogs spend their lives in organised military dog platoons where all required comforts can be found. Large kennelling, relaxation areas, training facilities, healthcare and a nutritious diet are all provided. In each platoon a supervisor is assigned in order to look after the organisation, training and efficiency of that platoon.

The dogs' training continues in the unit under the supervisor's instructions so the teams can both increase their operational abilities and maintain them at a high level. Dogs continue their training throughout their lifetime. The supervisor of each unit works out a daily training program for each team to suit their requirements and abilities.

The armed forces obtain military dogs at one or two years old. They stay in service up to twelve years of age, the maximum age of retirement. Dogs that retire are given to the NCO guards with whom they formed a team, or are nursed up to their old age in the unit. A small cemetery is provided in each unit so that when dogs die, they are buried with respect for the services they offered for years.

Every year, each dog unit is surveyed and dog teams are evaluated. Each guard dog is expected to successfully complete a series of drills, tests and scenarios to remain operational. The overall running of the military dogs in the Hellenic forces is set in the Air Force Regulations and Orders so that all actions and procedures concerning the use of military dogs are standardised for all three services.

Since 1989, when employment of military dogs began in the Air Force, 880 dogs in total have been trained for operational duties. An equivalent number has also been trained by the army. The majority of them are not currently in service as many have retired or died; the exact operational number is classified.

TURKEY

Within the Turkish armed forces' dog training school there are six different branches: mine-search dogs, bomb-search dogs, search and rescue dogs, tracking dogs, patrol dogs and the joint training wing.

Mine detection dogs (MDDs) were first used in 1981. The mine-dog breeds are labrador retrievers and German shepherds.

Bomb-dog training was established in 1995. Training explosive detection dogs (EDDs) is a long process with only the best dogs qualifying. Standards are very high and dogs are put through rigorous exercise, including regular introduction of new items and odours. The qualifications necessary for the dogs is a high level of intelligence, sound temperament and, to a lesser degree, aggression. After the basic training, they undertake advanced search education, strengthening the ability of the dog to respond to increasingly difficult types of targets. These include buildings, vehicles, aircraft, luggage and people.

Search and rescue dog training started in 1995. Search and rescue dogs are trained to locate live or injured parties in open land or forested areas, or via avalanche detection in natural disasters such as landslides and floods.

In ideal conditions, tracker dogs can follow a person with a track up to twelve hours old and can detect a person's scent 5,000 metres (3 miles) away.

Patrol dogs are also known as reconnaissance dogs. Their sense of smell is used when securing an area to provide detection and warning of the existence or approach the enemy. The breeds of dogs used are German shepherds, Belgian malinois and Turkey shepherds.

Finally, the joint training wing is responsible for socialisation training, obedience training and advanced obedience training programs.

Natural Disaster Search and Rescue Command Battalion (DAK)

DAK was established and equipped to international standard in the wake of several devastating earthquakes in Turkey. The Turkish government needed international assistance after these events, which came from Israel, the United States and Greece. Recently a twelve-strong team of Turkish army rescuers joined 12 Greek air force experts, firefighters and special forces to practice using sound detectors and sniffer dogs to locate buried victims in case of a strong earthquakes.

DAK responds to earthquakes, fires, floods, avalanches, landslides, incidents of large loss of life, and major accidents in all weather and field conditions, both at home and abroad.

In the early morning hours on 17 August 1999, northwestern Turkey was hit by an earthquake of 7.4 on the Richter scale, which lasted 45 seconds. At daybreak Turkey was confronted by a new reality. Tens of thousands of buildings had collapsed; oil refineries were ablaze; and tens of thousands of people were missing. The Turkish authorities had appealed for help to the international community, and foreign rescue missions began pouring into Turkey.

Israel's Prime Minister and the acting Minister of Security Ehud Barak had instructed the Home Front Command to prepare to launch a rescue mission. The first Israeli rescue team had landed on Turkish soil in the late afternoon and was assigned by the Turkish authorities to undertake rescue operations on the naval base at the town of Gulcuk. When the dimensions of the disaster became apparent, two more Israeli rescue teams, including search and rescue dogs and a field hospital unit, were dispatched to Turkey. The DAK was established from this model.

Within the Natural Disasters Search and Rescue Battalion, Battalion Headquarters, six DAK rescue dog sections are available. Each section has a commander who is a professional dog trainer, plus six dog teams, totalling seven staff with three search dogs per section.

DAK dogs are highly trained and operate in all terrains and extreme environments. Teams can be sent to search collapsed buildings, using their dogs to listen for the heartbeat of humans or the slightest movements. Similarly, DAK dogs can work in deep snow conducting avalanche search operations.

Water is no obstacle to DAK dog teams as they are trained to search for missing persons in lakes, rivers and marshland. The dogs can be placed at the front of a boat to detect the scent of humans, like US navy dogs in Vietnam.

SPAIN

Within the Spanish Ministry of Defence (MoD), dogs are divided into the following units: the Royal Guard, the army, navy (Marines), air force,

Emergency Military Unit, the School Cinológica of Defense, The Civil Guard and National Intelligence Centre.

Royal Guard

The Royal Guard is a military unit whose mission is to provide military guard service and escorts to His Majesty the King and members of the royal family.

Within the Royal Guards is a company of military dog handlers. The dog handler section is commanded by a lieutenant and has 60 dogs, most of which are explosive detectors. A quarter are attack dogs and generally a maximum of five drug-sniffing dogs are in the unit.

Army

The focus of MWD use is in the army, where most of the dogs within the MoD are employed. There are two groups of dogs: specialty detection and guards. The specialty dogs, with more than 100 dogs, are deployed throughout the country at different bases and barracks. There are also security dogs, drug detectors and EDD teams currently on UN missions in Lebanon. A section in the MP battalion operate drug detection and EDDs.

The guard and sentry MWDs within the army total more than 500 dogs trained to bark when an intruder approaches, and bite if it crosses the boundaries or on command. They are used to protect ammunition dumps, water tanks, military bases or any other facility that is considered a sensitive target.

A Spanish Army MWD was recently awarded the UN Medal for pPeace in Lebanon. The dog, Arno, was symbolically decorated for his lifesaving work in the service of soldiers. Arno, who belongs to the Military Police Unit Cordobesa Brigade, is part of the UN Interim Force in southern Lebanon (UNIFIL). The eight-year-old Belgian-bred malinois specialises in detecting explosives hidden in vehicles and performs its task with another dog at the entrance to the base Miguel de Cervantes, the headquarters of the eastern sector of UNIFIL under Spanish control. This is the second mission Arno has been deployed to in Lebanon.

Navy

In the navy all dog units are part of the Marines. Within the Marine Corps is the Force Protection Group, which is in charge of security at the bases of the navy. In total there are more than 100 naval MWDs with the three specialties in similar proportions: security and combat, drug-detection and explosive-detection. The explosive ordnance demolition (EOD) unit in the navy has dog support provided by the Marines for EDD means.

Air Force

The air force has two types of MWDs. The first is patrol dogs stationed at air bases. Each of the five bases has fourteen patrol dogs. The other group is at the School of Defense and Security Technical Support with more than 60 dogs. The school is responsible for the renewal and training of the dogs at air bases. The air force maintains a small number of EDDs for its own use.

Emergency Military Unit

The mission of this unit is to search for and rescue missing persons in large open areas, snow avalanches and disasters of every kind. Dogs are deployed if any of these emergency situations occur. This unit is deployed throughout the national territory and has prepared teams of dogs to locate victims buried under rubble, victims in large urban areas or missing persons in forest areas.

School Cinológica of Defense

By order of the Logistics Division of the Army in 1982, the operational Breeding and Training Centre for Dogs was established in Carabanchel Alto (Madrid). In 2002 the Centre of Veterinary Military Defence was established. In 2008 the structure was renamed Cinológica School of Defence. The school is the focal point for all matters relating to the acquisition, breeding, training, instruction, education, registration and control of dogs under the MoD.

There is a total of 120 dogs. Forty of these dogs belong to the groups operating from the school. These groups are the drug-detection, explosives- and mine-detection, security and combat search and rescue. The remaining dogs are for students of various courses offered by the school. It also provides dogs for guard and sentry dogs and to replenish the different armies upon request. Currently the school has deployed EDD teams on NATO missions and in Afghanistan.

Civil Guard

In 1982 the Civil Guard Service Cinológica was created in order to support the operational units of the corps by providing technical and specific support for such tasks as such as searching for missing persons, disaster intervention, drug interdiction and explosives search, mountain rescues and any other special mission. The primary objective remains law enforcement and protecting the freedoms and guarantee of public security. Civil Guard dogs are distributed throughout the national territory, mainly located in ports, airports, prisons and in capitals of autonomous regions.

The Civil Guard is a military unit with similar police missions to the French gendarmerie. It has a dog training school and distributes handlers all across Spain. The Civil Guard has its own school which is responsible for teaching expertise to staff being integrated into canine operational units. In addition, the school is tasked to train instructors for dog training.

ITALY

The Army Group Cinofilo (Dog Battalion) was established on 1 July 2002 in Grosseto. The battalion is unique, with its own command, and organised specifically to ensure both the breeding of dogs and the training of combinations in different specialisations. They are also responsible for both the training and operational employment of military dogs. Its core task is developing dogs for use with Italian forces abroad, but they may be employed in Italian territory for strategic objectives such as searching for weapons, ammunition and explosives.

Historically, dogs were often used alongside Italian armies. The Romans used them against many enemies, including Celtic tribes, Greeks and fellow Romans. At the beginning of the 20th century, like many European armies, Italy began using war dogs: not only in combat but also in diverse and complex tasks such as health care. They were used in World War I as sentinels in the Balkans and Tripoli. During World War II Italian forces used dogs to guard prisoners of war and vital assets, such as railheads and bridges in the country.

The insignia of the Italian Army Group Cinofilo summarises the particular nature of the unit that is not characterised by specific features of their own. Indeed, the personnel belonging to the department come from all branches and corps of the army and only once they have gained the specialisation of dog handler are they allocated to the engineer regiment. The insignia is composed of a dog's head and the sword and the blaze of the sappers.

The method of training used by the military instructors does not include coercive procedures. Encouragement is the preferred method; all training activities are aimed at strengthening the bond of affection, feelings of mutual trust, understanding and teamwork between the dog and its handler. Games plays a central role in training the dog, which learns to recognise and indicate on any type of explosives.

The dog specialisation course is available after an initial course, lasting about a year, involving the conduct of specific activities to give the dogs combat capability with such skills as transportation to any tactical military vehicle, passing a watercourse, techniques of movement and combat in an urban environment, patrolling sensitive areas, crowd control, gun steadiness, automatic immediate response procedures and much more.

The program for explosive detection has worked well enough to arouse the interest of overseas armies, who more than once have chosen to send handlers to the Italian Army Group Cinofilo for joint training. On completion of each course, on-the-job training is conducted for around a month in Kosovo. The Task Force Ercole has the duty of drilling various dog teams in order to reach a high level of mission capability. The drills include canine units of the Operational Company of the Task Force Star, who work permanently in Kosovo with four dog teams, or Task Force Aquila, which comes from Grosseto.

This training form teams of MDDs and EDDs. The MDDs will be used to clear minefields or to evacuate the wounded inside these fields. The EDDs use scent to verify the presence of explosives or booby-traps in buildings and to prevent illegal transportation of explosives with controls on vehicles at checkpoints.

Today the air force, as well as the Italian army, field a number of dog handlers protecting both domestic military and international interest on operational deployments.

Among the different breeds of suitable military dogs, the air force has predominantly chosen German shepherds. This breed has proved to be the most versatile for training, with its obedience, balance between docility and aggression, considerable learning ability, strength and stamina, courage, intelligence, great capacity in scenting and extreme loyalty.

Explosive Ordnance Disposal (EOD)

The dog platoon EOD unit, consisting of a volunteer sapper EOD first level and a dog trained at the Department of Grosseto, are tasked with the detection of explosive ordnance and can perform tasks such as recognition of weapons. A dog EOD platoon consists of a core command, EOD teams and four dogs. Each team, led by a sergeant, comprises three core dog handlers equipped with EOD equipment and a system for the detection of mines.

Scout Dog

Dog handlers are responsible for searching for previously identified elements of the enemy (tracking), detection of booby traps, minefields and explosive devices hidden on the ground, with dogs indicating their presence silently.

The most important defence mechanism of a scout dog is that its senses are more developed than those of humans, particularly its smell and hearing. If thoroughly trained and employed in ideal conditions, on average, a search dog is able to sense odours and sounds 40 times better than a man.

Security and Surveillance

Dog handlers of the Security and Vigilance platoons are used to increase the security level of a command, as part of a surveillance and security system. Dogs are employed in static or mobile patrols. Selected dogs also have the ability to detect explosives, and therefore can be used to prevent criminal activity, particularly in the fight against terrorism. Dogs are used on vehicle checkpoints to supervise the movement of staff and vehicles in and out of bases. They are best employed at night or in poor visibility, where their enhanced senses are best utilised. Security dogs are used for the protection of VIPs and vital facilities.

Many Italian dogs have seen operational action in such places as Kosovo, Iraq and Afghanistan. Many have received awards for their bravery and life-saving skills.

Brando, a six-year-old male German shepherd, is a wonderful example. He was specialised as a patrol dog and was then trained to perform in territorial control operations in high-intensity scenarios. Brando may in fact be considered a true sensor; thanks to his extraordinary olfactory and auditory abilities, he can be used both for searching for any type of explosive and for the supervision of points and sensitive areas. In Afghanistan, while seconded for two weeks at the base Delaram in Farah province, he identified a dangerous explosive device that was readily neutralised. For this reason he was awarded a medal in Rome in the presence of the president of the republic.

Megane is the first dog to have been qualified as a military mine detection dog. A seven-year-old female German shepherd, she is very exuberant, with a great desire to play; when there is a job to do, however, she is transformed: no technology can compete with her exceptional sense of smell. She is able to reclaim areas and potentially dangerous routes in next to no time, avoiding the risks of mine accidents. Her professional career has included many missions abroad, such as Enduring Freedom in 2004. Posted in Khost Province in Afghanistan, she has been widely used in the reconnaissance of routes in one of the highest-density landmine areas in the world.

Fidji is a young, strong Belgian malinois. He is a specialised scout dog and, as such, has been trained to move ahead on a patrol to prevent ambushes. In the presence of specific indications on the ground, Fidji is able to verify the route and report the presence of mines, booby traps and other types of hidden weapons.

California is a female four-year-old Doberman who was trained to find explosives. Only one year out of training, she already has been used once in Kosovo and is on her second mission in Lebanon. During one of the checks of vehicles entering the base of Tibnin, where the Italian contingent is located, she found explosives hidden in a truck.

Handlers are responsible for the care, training and employment in operations of the dog. A good handler must have a dog-loving set of qualities, which includes a balanced sense of responsibility, motivation and enthusiasm, and a natural predisposition to work with dogs.

Progress in training with the dog involves constant work, characterised by calm, consistency, communication skills and concentration. The best handlers are always relaxed and patient, able to motivate their dog at the right time, able to understand the causes of an error and to recognise what stimulates their dog work. It's obvious that beyond these natural qualities, an Italian dog handler requires thorough knowledge and expertise acquired only through long and demanding training, a steady job and vital experience in daily operations.

Italian Gendarmie

The *Arma dei Carabinieri* (Carabinieri Corps) is the national gendarmerie of Italy, policing both the military and civilian populations. The Carabinieri were raised in status and became an armed force on 31 March, 2000 (alongside the army, navy and air force); prior to this it was part of the army. The Carabinieri, including military dog teams, perform Military Police (MP) and security duties for the Ministry of Defence, military high commands, offices of the military judiciary and allied military organisations in Italy and abroad.

During World War II, they fought as MP against the allied forces and against Yugoslav Partisans as part of the Italian occupation force in Yugoslavia. In recent years Carabinieri units have been dispatched on peacekeeping missions, including Kosovo, Afghanistan and Iraq. In 2003 twelve Carabinieri were killed in a suicide bombing on their base in Nasiriyah, near Basra, southern Iraq, constituting the largest Italian military loss of life in a single action since World War II.

PORTUGAL

Since the early days of its existence, the Battalion of Paratrooper Hunters has tried to implement a unit of combat dogs within their structure. On 7 June 1956, the Command called to the BCP CITFA (Battalion Of Hunters Parachute, Education and Training Command Air Forces) established the provisions, training manuals and guidelines on the treatment of war dogs. They based these on guidelines from the British army.

The efforts of the BCP command were eventually rewarded on 4 July 1957, when the Secretary of State for Air Force made the following order: 'The Battalion of Hunters paratroops is to establish kennels that are intended to provide dogs not only for that unit but for all of the Air Force.'

The Centre for Investigation and Filing of Military Dogs (CIDCM) was created to oversee military dog requirements for paratroopers and also provide dogs to ensure the security of air bases, thus minimising the number of operational staff required in the overseas provinces.

Some important milestones in the history of MWDs in Portugal are:

• The construction of kennels was considered an absolute priority. The enthusiasm and commitment of General Kaúlza de Arriaga made it possible by May 1958.

• In 1958 the first dogs were purchased and shipped to Alsace in a Portuguese military plane from the Lahr base in Germany. This base was under French military occupation at the time, and all the dogs were bought from France and Germany. It was in France that Portuguese specialists first obtained the materials and techniques to be able to employ parachute-combat dogs.

• In December 1958 the commander of the battalion, Colonel Armindo Martins Videira disseminated 'the rules concerning the use of military dogs' to all units.

• At the Centre for Instruction and Storage of Military Dogs there were only ten dogs in April 1959. It was the need for new acquisitions that made it necessary to build some infrastructure essential for expanding operations, such as quarantine facilities, a kitchen, an infirmary, fields of education and a secretary.

• The first public appearance of the combat dogs was in June 1959, with the participation of the battalion in the 52nd International Dog Exhibition in Lisbon, held at the city zoo.

• The first jump of a dog in a parachute from the skies of Tancos took place in February 1960.

• The first use of dogs in combat was in the end of 1960 in Luanda, where a combat dog detachment was sent to ensure the safety of air base No.9. They were also used in the role of public order maintenance due to riots in the Angolan capital.

• In March 1961, defenceless farms in northern Angola were brutally attacked by the Union of Angolan Peoples (UPA). The Portuguese government thus sent the 1st CPC, the 2nd CPC, and later the 3rd CPC to Angola. They were accompanied by a detachment of combat dogs.

• The dog section expanded to 60 dogs in 1963.

• In 1963 a detachment of combat dogs was sent to reinforce a platoon of BCP to maintain the security of Aerodrome Base 2 in Bissalanca.

The airborne troops were pioneers in the use of military dogs in Portugal. During the Portuguese Colonial War in Africa between 1961 and 1974, military dogs were used in the areas of custody facilities and detection of mines and patrols. This provided a basis for other corps of military and security forces to develop and implement MWD programs.

After the war overseas, military dogs were of great use in the units. For many years they were used in public skydiving displays, to guard facilities, in parades, to detect drugs (often used by new recruits) and explosives, and in joint operations with other battalions.

Budgetary restrictions and a review of the tasks attributed to the airborne troops forced a rethink of the presence of military dogs. Thus, in 1990, the CCTP (Command Corps of Airborne Troops) decided to start the process of removing military dogs from its order of battle. At that time military kennel installations for dogs were reduced in space by 50 per cent.

For some years, their use was confined largely to guarding installations. In S. Jacinto, the Section of Military Dogs closed in May 1994 and a Centre for Dogs only remained in Tancos. The dog unit developed interesting activities, including the parachute jump dog display teams. Several times, these teams were also requested by civil authorities to aid in the detection of missing persons, with remarkable success.

On 5 March 2008 the War Dog Section was reopened in S. Jacinto Cinotécnicas with four teams (two male and two female handlers) newly arrived from Afghanistan.

Today, dogs of war have returned to their specialist airborne troop role. They are prepared to intervene in peacekeeping missions or conflict all over the world and are finally expanding in numbers again.

MIDDLE EAST

ISRAEL

IDF Elite Oketz Unit

Unit Oketz is an independent canine Special Forces (*sayeret*) unit, initially founded in 1939 as part of the Haganah, used for perimeter security of villages under threat from their Arab neighbours. In 1948, following the establishment of the state, the unit joined the Israel Defence Forces (IDF) and set up its base in Kiryat Haim. In 1954 the unit was disbanded and, twenty years later, was re-established under the command of the chief infantry officer.

Selection into this elite unit is a long process. To get accepted, soldiers need to pass gruelling stamina tests. Once in, they undergo full combat basic training, just like their infantry counterparts. The unit specialises in training and handling dogs for military applications. Each dog is trained for a particular specialty. Attack dogs are trained to operate in urban areas, as well as in rural and bush land (they were used extensively in Lebanon). Dogs are trained in tracking for manhunts and detecting breaches at the borders. Dogs are also trained to search for guns and munitions. Explosives dogs sniff out hidden explosives, and search and rescue dogs find people in collapsed buildings.

Oketz is one of the most highly regarded of the army's units, and few infantry commanders would even think about embarking on a mission without their support. Today, almost every arrest operation is led by Oketz.

Oketz operators are often assigned to other units in the case of a particular need for their specialist skills, such as in the extraction of terrorists from fortified buildings. Though not affiliated with the IDF Paratroopers Brigade, Unit Oketz operators wear the same distinctive red berets and the unit's graduation ceremony is held at paratroopers headquarters.

Since 2002, soldiers and dogs from Oketz have been able to prevent at least 200 suicide attacks in the central region. In 2006 alone Oketz dogs participated in more than 4,000 operations. Every day, some twelve dogs are out in the field participating in various operations on all of Israel's fronts: Gaza, West Bank and the northern border with Lebanon.

Dogs participate in counter-terror raids in every major operation. There are two options: either a soldier searches the house or a dog does. Using a dog minimises collateral damage, harm to innocent civilians and damage to infrastructure. This is also why Oketz's real strengths and advantages can only really be felt in asymmetrical warfare and low-intensity conflict, and not during a large-scale conventional conflict.

The use of dogs by the military has been a sensitive subject, as they were associated with Nazi attack dogs in the minds of many Jews. For a long time the unit's existence was kept secret so as not to offend survivors of the Holocaust who will never forget the images of Nazi soldiers unleashing their dogs. Their use on missions against the Palestinians is also controversial, with dogs being largely reviled by Arabs. But Israel is now willing to trumpet its achievements, claiming that dogs have been responsible for saving many hundreds of lives.

In 1988 the unit participated in IDF operations in southern Lebanon. The operation was launched to destroy the cave-based headquarters of the Popular Front for the Liberation of Palestine in a mountainous area 20 kilometres (12.4 miles) south of Beirut. Golani Brigade soldiers, naval commandos and a number of Oketz dogs participated in the operation, after which the canine unit was revealed to the public for the first time. In the Second Lebanon War, Oketz accompanied Golani and Paratrooper units inside southern Lebanon when searching Hizbullah underground bunker systems locating weaponry and terrorists.

A vivid symbol of the relationship between Unit Oketz's warriors and their dogs is the unit's canine graveyard, formed to honour the memory of the dogs that fell in the line of duty. The cemetery at the Oketz Military Base in central Israel is the final resting place of 60 four-legged recruits. It bears testimony to the increasingly significant role that dogs have come to play in the ranks of the military. Amid the tombstones stands a large sculpture of a dog and handler with an inscription reading: 'Walk softly, for here lie soldiers of Israel.'

Unit policy is that any dog that loses its life in the line of duty receives a military funeral. Every year, on the eve of Independence Day, a remembrance ceremony is held for the dogs that have died in action.

Dogs in the Unit

Unit Oketz prefers malinois over German shepherds and Rottweilers, which were formerly employed. The reasons for the choice are twofold: they're the perfect size to be picked up by their handler, while still being able to attack an enemy, and their coats are short and generally fair in colour, making them less prone to heatstroke.

Dogs are recruited eighteen 18 months of age and put through a rapid screening process and basic training before being matched up with an individual soldier. The dogs will then be taught skills ranging from sniffing out survivors of earthquakes to detecting hidden caches of arms and explosives.

While a dog has long been known as man's best friend, in the Oketz that saying takes on a new meaning. Soldiers grow up with their dogs, and they undergo eighteen months of training together before being deployed in the field. After six years of service, the dogs are retired and placed in the hands of former members of the unit, who are queuing up to take care of them.

The Oketz base, located at the Adam training facility near Modi'in, looks like any other base. At the top of a winding hill are the kennels. Needless to say, the dogs don't appreciate unfamiliar visitors. Each block within the kennel is reserved for the four specific types of dogs: search and rescue, attack, bomb detection or tracking. They also spend much of their time in a specially designed sports centre, that comes equipped with treadmills to build up their stamina.

Beyond their bomb detection capabilities, there are additional advantages to using dogs in operations. Dogs move fast and quietly. If you want to sneak up on someone, or if you are engaging a hidden infiltrator, the dog can cancel out the element of surprise. The unit's slogan—'At the front'—perfectly describes the role handlers and their dogs play during a mission.

Israel Border Guards

There are several other para-military organisations within Israel that use dogs in combative roles.

The total number of border guards is believed to be about 6,000 soldiers and officers. Because of their combat training, border policemen are employed in unquiet areas, where there are greater risks for riots, violence and even terrorism. They serve mainly in the countryside, at Arab villages and towns (along with the regular police), and near the borders and at the West Bank. Serving three years as a border policeman is equal to three years as an IDF soldier. All border policemen receive combat training and are additionally trained for counter-terrorism, riot control and police work. The best candidates are selected to specialise in and receive training to become dog operators.

Security-obsessed Israel is rolling out stringent measures for the pontiff's pilgrimage to the Holy Land, with tens of thousands of law enforcement officers deployed, entire sections of Jerusalem to be shut down at various times and Israeli air space to be closed for the papal arrival as part of Operation White Robe.

Special Police Unit

The Yamam is, in Hebrew, the acronym for Special Police Unit, Israel's elite civilian police counter-terrorism unit. The Yamam answers to the Israel Border Police central command and belongs to the civilian Israel police forces rather than the military. The Yamam is capable of both hostage-rescue operations and offensive takeover raids against targets in civilian areas. Besides military duties, it also performs SWAT duties and undercover police work. The Yamam is self-dependent, training its own operators in all fields, such as sniping, reconnaissance and dog operation.

Search and Rescue

The function of the Home Front Command's Search and Rescue unit is intended 'for performance of distinct S&R missions in the country as well as abroad, in peacetime, in war and in emergency, anyplace and at any time as needed'. The unit combines all the specialist units that are involved with search and rescue. The unit has participated in many special search and rescue operations, both in Israel and abroad.

There are only a few search and rescue dogs in the unit, due to their special nature and complex training requirements. These dogs are used around the country to assist in dozens of search operations, including searching for senior citizens, Alzheimer's Disease sufferers and people with suicidal tendencies who have gone missing. The unit, which carries out joint exercises with the IDF's elite Oketz canine unit, is ready to move anywhere in the country.

A search and rescue dog can identify the scent of a person in distress or a dead person (up to 48 hours after death) from a considerable distance. The dog can distinguish between the scent emitted by someone stationary (the missing person) and that of someone moving (the search team), even at night. As soon as the dog identifies the scent, he will lead the dog handler to its source, sit down and bark. These dogs are capable of locating a dead body in just five minutes in a 500 square metre (0.3 square miles) area, even in stony, difficult terrain that is not reachable by the search team.

ARAB NATIONS

Sniffer dogs are universally recognised as the most effective means of detecting explosives. But in Iraq, as in much of the Arab world, dogs are considered unclean. One of the most useful security tools is a difficult one for Iraqis to accept because of this cultural taboo. However, with the assistance of foreign powers and education of the Iraqi military on the effectiveness of dogs, the Iraqi government has instituted a MWD program.

The army and the para-military police force are training both explosive detection dogs and general purpose patrol dogs. These dogs will eventually perform functions within the military, border patrol and law enforcement areas. One of the ways the Iraqi army has seen the value of MWDs is by joint patrols with US forces. Seeing firsthand how effective dogs can be on patrols has caused Iraqi commanders to seek their own MWD assets.

Recently the Croatian army trained several specialist EDD teams for Iraqi forces. Iraq has requested an estimated 600 further MWDs from United Nations sources. It is believed that the preferred suppliers are Croatia and South Africa.

The Iraqi National Canine Program in Baghdad program is slated to expand to include 100 dogs and their handlers. Iraqi police dogs often help maintain security at Shaab stadium in Baghdad ahead of soccer matches between the Iraqi and Palestinian teams, where passions often run high. The police force dog teams are trained by military coalition forces.

ASIA

CHINA

The Chinese Army (People's Liberation Army, PLA) has used military working dogs (MWDs) to quell public demonstrations. PLA dogs have been seen during high-profile security operations, such as the Olympic Games. The army uses dogs extensively on the borders between China and Russia.

To meet the PLA's needs for grassroots military dog management, a military dog magazine was recently officially published and circulated. The monthly magazine is run by the Organisation and Discipline Department of the Headquarters of the Beijing Military Area Command under the entrustment of the General Staff Headquarters of the PLA.

All three services use MWDs. The PLA navy uses guard dogs to secure facilities and bases. The Air Force uses them in base protection as well as explosive detection, while the Army is the largest user of MWDs in specialist roles and general patrol tasks. China has also recently established a search and rescue dog unit, mainly due to recent major natural disasters throughout the country and, to some extent, by observing many international agencies' use of SAR dogs sent to China as part of United Nations assistance programs.

The Chinese police use dogs for law enforcement and security functions, including border patrol. At present, there are 4,000 police dogs, 408 units with police dogs, and 4,300 police dog technical personnel all over the country. Police dog techniques are widely used in public security, such as searching for narcotics, tracking, scent identification, searching for and apprehending suspects, searching for explosives, controlling and preventing violence, and patrolling.

At the request of the United Nations and approved by the Central Military Commission, the fifth detachment of the Chinese peacekeeping engineering battalion to Lebanon was officially formed on 20 January 2009 from an engineering regiment of the Chengdu Military Area Command stationed in Yunan Province. The advanced echelon of the fifth detachment left China for Lebanon in mid-February and the second echelon left in late March. The main equipment and materials, including the dogs, were freighted to Lebanon by sea. The battalion organised pertinent training tasks before going abroad, such as peacekeeping operation, field first aid, barracks defense and canine minesweeping and explosive detection drills.

The People's Armed Police (PAP) is the para-military force primarily responsible for law enforcement and internal security and is under a unique dual-leadership system of the Central Military Commission and local police departments. The PAP was formed in 1983 when the PLA transferred its internal security and border defence responsibilities to this unit. It is in this peacetime role that the PAP relies heavily on the use of dogs, especially along the border areas. These dogs patrol in extreme environmental conditions, from high-altitude mountainous terrain to the searing heat of the Gobi Desert. In wartime, the PAP would be used as light infantry, performing border defense and other support functions to assist the regular ground forces.

The Snow Wolf Commando Unit (SWRU) is a special police unit of the People's Republic of China tasked with counter-terrorism, riot control, and other special tasks, such as anti-hijacking and bomb disposal. The SWRU, along with the PAP, was tasked with many of the security responsibilities for the 2008 Summer Olympics. The unit makes extensive use of both attack dogs and explosive-detection dogs (EDDs).

INDIA

India, one of the world's largest operators of MWDs, has a dog army of several thousand specialised canines. The predominant breeds are mostly labradors, German shepherds and Belgian malinois. The success rate against the militants has increased with the use of military dogs, and now virtually every unit deployed in counter-insurgency operations has a dog unit. Dogs have proved lifesavers for the forces in many instances, as they have led patrols to deeply buried explosives and mines in the northeast as well as in Jammu and Kashmir. Naturally these jobs aren't without their share of risks; dogs spotted by insurgents are often shot.

Labradors, who have an uncanny sense of sniffing out militants, now lead all anti-militancy and road-opening missions in Jammu and Kashmir. German shepherd and Belgian malinois dogs are not far behind and form the bulwark of army mine and explosive hunting missions. The Indian army states that dogs are a force multiplier in counter-insurgency operations in the northeast, and Jammu and Kashmir. Last year, six dogs were deployed to the deep jungles in Chhattisgarh. In three months they did what the rest of the army couldn't in ten years: locating Naxalite hideouts, training areas and ammunition caches.

It is due to this success that there is virtually a clamour from para-military forces for such trained dogs. According to rough estimates, dogs have been useful in more than 300 anti-militancy encounters over the years. Besides this, the dogs were successful in sniffing out explosives and mines in more than 110 instances in 2009.

The vital contribution of these dogs has been recognised and gave them pride of place in a public display at the Republic Day Parade and the Army Day Parade.

Specialist Explosive Detection Dogs (EDDs)

The army now has 85 specialised dog units, with each unit comprising 24 dogs. Of these, as many as 35 are deployed in Jammu and Kashmir, fifteen in the northeast and the remainder in the Western and Southern Army Commands. Search dogs have won as many as 29 special commendations from the Chief of the Army Staff, while their handlers have won three times as many such coveted awards. The dogs have even won overseas assignments, with almost all the 8,560 Indian troops deployed in UN peacekeeping missions sporting three to four dog units. The success rate is so high that twenty units have also been deployed all along the 743 kilometre- (461 mile-) long Line of Control in Jammu and Kashmir.

The Remount Veterinary Corps (RVC) traces its history as far back as 1779. The function of the Army Veterinary School is to train MWDs. The Dog Training Faculty came into existence as an integral part of the centre in 1960. In 2005 the RVC Centre and School was redesignated the RVC Centre and College.

The RVC Centre and College is the amalgamation of all RVC personnel. The centre imparts basic military and technical training to young veterinary graduates, as well as other technical trades, such as dressers, riders, army dog trainers, kennel-men, laboratory attendants, farriers and clerks.

The dog training wing of the RVC teaches basic canine obedience and advanced training to personnel and dogs in specialist tasks such as infantry patrolling, guarding, tracking, avalanche rescue, and explosive and mine detection. The scope of training has recently been expanded to search and rescue operations, crude oil leakage detection and detection of improvised explosive devices (IEDs).

The faculty is also responsible for the organisation of public dog demonstrations, the issue of trained dogs to various friendly foreign countries and the conduct of courses for officers who may lead MWD units. It is also responsible for the breeding and procurement of dogs to meet requirements for the army, air force, National Security Guards (NSG) and Special Frontier Force (SFF). Finally, the faculty is also charged with the holding and maintenance of reserve army dogs and issuing them to regular army dog units as required.

Today roughly, 60 per cent of India's dog troops are composed of labradors; the rest are mostly German shepherds. A few Belgian malinois—imported from Austria ten years ago—have also been deployed. But though these are a hardy, powerful breed, and a hit with the police and army in the UK and US, their violent streak and inability to get used to more than one master make them less than ideal for Indian conditions. The army also experimented with boxers, which they rejected as physically unfit for duty, and Dobermans, which were dismissed from service twenty years ago.

Dogs are trained and assessed right from puppyhood at the RVC facility in Meerut cantonment in western Uttar Pradesh. Even as newly weaned six-week-olds, they undergo an aptitude test to assess their temperament and physical attributes. After six months' romping around in their play areas and squabbling over toys, the pups, along with their handlers, embark on a rigorous eight-month course to increase their agility and fitness. Most importantly, they are taught to understand, obey and trust their master's word of command. At the end of the course, the trainers at the dog faculty examine the meticulous progress reports maintained on each dog to see who will remain. Once divided into different squads according to their individual attributes, the dogs undergo intensive simulation training for about 36 weeks, in conditions close to those they will eventually have to work in (EDD, tracker, guard, infantry patrol, and search and rescue).

In 2009, after observing the success of dogs in detecting explosives planted by militants in Kashmir, the Indian army decided to raise additional dog squads to detect high- and low-grade explosives, metallic and plastic mines. A study carried out by army experts revealed that detection of explosives by dogs has an 84 per cent success rate. The detection of explosives by soldiers is 32 per cent, while detection of explosives by sophisticated methods is 48 per cent. A senior Indian army officer recently said that the services rendered by dogs in detecting ambush sites, snipers, enemy hideouts, arms caches and infiltration has been a remarkable feat. The dogs are able to detect explosives concealed in suitcases, boxes, pressure cookers and cylinders. They can also detect transient human bombs because of their higher sense of discrimination.

Soldiers count on dogs for sanitising buildings, vehicles, roads and helipads. They have the capacity to track for 6-8 kilometres (4-5 miles) on a 24-48-hour-old scent and can pick up any sound or movement up to 200 metres (0.1 miles).

PAKISTAN

The Army Dog Breeding Centre and Training School (ADBTC&S) was established in 1952. It was assigned the mission of breeding, rearing, training and issuing trained dogs to various formations and units. In addition, the school was also responsible for training the officers and soldiers in different dog courses. Initially, 114 people and 292 dogs were authorised on its establishment. In 1965, the unit was reduced to sixteen people and 63 dogs, but in 1966-1967 the Table of Organisation and Equipment was revised and the school's strength was increased to 50 people and 100 dogs. In 1986, the numbers increased again to 102 people and 300 dogs.

The school is situated at a distance of 4 kilometres (2.5 miles) from Rawalpindi Railway Station and approximately 10 kilometres (6 miles) from Islamabad Airport. This is an ideal training area to get dogs used to all possible tactical conditions, such as mountainous or desert regions. From April to September the minimum temperature remains up to 26°C while the maximum goes up to 45°C. From October to March the minimum temperature is -3°C and the maximum up to 28°C.

The school has a field demonstration area, aircraft search training at nearby army and air force bases, building, ground and vehicle search training areas, dog agility training facilities and tracking areas.

Time and again, dogs have proven to be one of the major assets for Pakistan's armed forces, police, customs and other associated organisations.

Sri Lanka

Dogs were a significant part of the success of the Sri Lankan army in the Eelam War. The army employs 75 dogs, which are among the most experienced in the world after their recent roles in detecting mines, explosives and warning soldiers against ambush. Dogs were much feared by Tamil Tiger insurgents.

South East Asia

Malaysia

The Malaysian Army War Dogs Wing was organised in 1957 by the British Army (Jungle Warfare School). On 4 November 1971, the wing was officially recognised and established with Major Arthur Gordon Wilder from the Royal Army Veterinary Corps (RAVC) United Kingdom as the first Officer Commanding.

In February 1972, tracking dogs were deployed to assist operations for the first time in east Malaysia. The success of the dogs in tracking the enemy and searching for booby traps was recognised by other troops in the United Nations operations. In the 1980s Malaysian military dogs were trained by the Australian Army to detect mines. Seven members of the Malaysian army undertook a three-month course at Holsworthy, New South Wales, Australia.

Dogs were fully utilised to combat the communist terrorists until 1989 when the they laid down their arms. The wing gradually expanded in size over the years to its current level, which consists of four officers and 135 other ranks, with 97 war dogs.

War dogs are trained for guarding, tracking and explosive searching. The roles of the war dog wing are to train war dogs and handlers, and operational duties.

The Philippines

The Armed Forces of the Philippines (AFP) Canine Company was activated on 4 February 2000. Situated at General Headquarters and Headquarters Service Command, Armed Forces Philippines (AFP) at Camp General Emilio Aguinaldo, Quezon City.

In the year 2000 the Philippines was shocked by numerous bombing incidents, particularly in the rural areas of Mindanao. A government statement declared: 'Due to wide violence that continuously terrorises the community, the Armed Forces of the Philippines conclusively created a new piece of valuable equipment which successfully descended insurgence through deterring acts of uprising individuals that generally affects the community and the entire nation.'

A new breed of weaponry against terrorism was born, which ultimately justified the friendship between man and dog. As partners, they became vital instruments for serenity and peace.

Their mission is to conduct MWD operations in support of the AFP Internal Security Operations. This includes:
- conducting sweeping and reconnaissance of concealed/buried explosives
- conducting surveillance, tracking and patrolling of suspected and/or identified insurgents and/or enemies of the state
- assisting in AFP special security operations

In August 2009 two canine teams successfully recovered 32 sacks of ammonium nitrate explosives, 828 dynamite sticks and 300 pieces of blasting caps at a routine vehicle checkpoint. The explosives were hidden in the truck under food sacks and box containers that were being transported to Surigao City, Mindanao.

Thailand

According to official Thai military doctrine, the military dog program in Thailand was first initiated by His Majesty King Bhumibol Adulyadej. The program was established in 1968 under the responsibility and supervision of the Office of the Supreme Commander, Royal Thai Armed Forces, which later delegated the task of operations to the Directorate of Joint Operations. The program was intended as a pilot project lasting five years.

In the beginning, the United States helped by providing seventeen German shepherds (two males and fifteen females) for breeding. A site of approximately 16 hectares was chosen in a forested area in Pak Chong district, Nakhon Ratchasima province to be the headquarters. The pilot project, which started off with just thirty officers and nine dogs, proved very successful. His Majesty King Bhumibol Adulyadej visited the site in 10 June 1972 and honoured all the graduated officers with War Dogs medals.

In 22 June 1973, upon the approval by the Ministry of Defence, the Military Dog Centre was established on a permanent basis. It comprised the commanding and administration offices, training school, veterinary hospital and breeding unit, together with 763 officers. On 1 February 1985, the Military Dog Centre was transferred to the jurisdiction of the Veterinary and Remount Department, Royal Thai Army.

The Military Dog Centre has been tasked with producing (with the general capacity of 180 puppies per year) and training military dogs for various official military missions, including border patrol and demarcation, mine detection and clearance (in cooperation with Thailand Mine Action Centre), discovering victims of natural disasters, bomb detection and general security operations. War dogs are used by all services in the Thai military.

At present the types of military working dogs on active service include German shepherds, labradors, Dobermans and Rottweilers. The Military Dog Centre also trains an indigenous domestic breed with a appearance similar to that of an Australian dingo.

SINGAPORE

The Singapore Armed Forces (SAF) established the first-of-its-kind SAF Dog Company in October 1970. These MWDs were trained as guard dogs to increase security for key SAF Camps. After 1971, its expansion led the company to be renamed the SAF Dog Unit.

Combat tracker dogs were introduced and trained in 1972, forming part of the combat tracker teams supporting infantry units. As the demand for MWDs increased and evolved, the SAF Dog Unit eventually became the SAF Dog Training School and commenced dog trainer and handler courses.

Countries around the world began utilising MWDs in more specialised operations, such as the detection of arms, explosives and narcotics. In keeping with the tide, the SAF soon established the Narcotics Detector Dog Section (NDD) in 1976 to counter drug trafficking, and it effectively reduced the use of narcotics by SAF servicemen. Operations were carried out in tandem with Military Police to enforce drug abuse and trafficking laws. The Arms and Explosive Dog Section (AES) was established to enhance the detection of substances that have traces of explosive chemicals, enabling the SAF to identify potential dangers early without risking the life of its soldiers.

In 2006, the SAF Dog Training School became the SAF Military Working Dog Unit (MWDU). Over the years, MWDU has developed and strengthened the role of MWDs across SAF. It has established numerous external dog detachments, housing more than 270 dogs and protecting vital installations. SAFPU also runs a veterinary clinic to provide necessary veterinary care. The clinic is staffed by both operationally ready national servicemen and full-time national servicemen.

Border controls are an important aspect of Singapore's national security. Since the terrorist attacks on the United States on 11 September 2001, security measures at Singapore's borders have been enhanced. As part of these security measures, an explosives ordnance disposal (EOD) team and arms and explosive search (AES) dogs are deployed at Woodlands Checkpoint, a critical node in Singapore's land access points. The AES dogs are trained to detect hidden arms and explosives. If such materials are found, the EOD team stationed at the checkpoint will neutralise them. Dog teams can be deployed to other land and sea access points when necessary.

Air Forces Security Guard Dogs

Singapore Air Forces Field Defence Squadrons (FDS) ensures the security of air bases through undertaking regular perimeter patrols and controlling personnel movement within the base.

Through regular training, the FDS is well prepared for its air base ground defence role. Part of FDS' assets at Sembawang air base are military working dogs. Recently, community leaders were treated to a demonstration by the FDS guard dogs, displaying their defence capabilities during a visit by the vice president. He was briefed on the key roles and responsibilities of the Island Defence Headquarters, which comprises the 2nd People's Defence Force (2 PDF) and agencies from the Ministry of Home Affairs.

The Island Defence Headquarters maintains a 24/7 national security watch, ready to respond decisively to any security threats to Singapore. Guard dogs are a key asset and force multiplier for home land security.

Vietnam

In 1961 the American Military Assistance Advisory Group, Vietnam, recommended that the South Vietnamese army (ARVN) use military working dogs for sentry and scout work. 300 dogs were purchased from Germany and shipped to the ARVN in mid-1962. The German-bred dogs were initially wary of the Vietnamese soldiers and barked or ran away from them.

Due to the cultural differences in how the Vietnamese viewed dogs compared with their US advisers, the project did not go well. The Vietnamese, as Buddhists, feared that by working with the dogs they would be reincarnated as dogs. They also refused to praise their dogs, which impeded the positive-based training practices that US- and German-bred dogs were used to. Finally, the physical condition of the dogs degenerated for several reasons. One was the fact that it would cost an ARVN soldier more to feed his dog each day than his family, so the dogs were often fed rice. Many dogs died of malnutrition. In 1964 the ARVN had 327 dogs and planned to employ over 1,000. By 1966, due to the above conditions, they had 130.

Today the Vietnamese Army uses dogs to guard installations and in the search and rescue role, having solved their past animal welfare issues due to a combination of animal welfare education and an appreciation of the abilities of MWDs.

Japan

Japan has a long history of employing MWDs. One of the earliest examples is dogs tracking down Russian prisoners of war in the Sino-Russian War. However, the akita dog of Japan is said to have guarded Samurai homes and used in the field to carry loads.

Japanese military dogs were used in Manchuria as messenger and guard dogs. During World War II, dogs were used in sentry roles, and it is believed attempts were made to train suicide dogs who would run towards enemy emplacements prior to exploding with a timed fuse.

Today the Japanese Self Defence Force (JSDF) employs MWDs in the Air Force Branch to guard bases.

SOUTH AMERICA

COLOMBIA

Many South American military departments have a unique dual status, with both federal and state missions. The federal mission is to maintain properly trained and equipped units for prompt federalisation in the event of war. State missions cover domestic emergencies (such as fighting major crime) or other emergencies (such as aid to civil power). Many South American police forces are para-military.

Latin American forces are seeking the support of Colombian dog experts to stop drug trafficking to Europe, through a specialised course financed by the European Commission and carried out by the Office of the UN against Drugs and Crime. The Colombian Police School is located at Facatativa, a municipality located 40 kilometres (25 miles) west of Bogota, Colombia.

Since the 1980s the United States has supported the fight against the drug war and cocaine production in several South American countries. The focus is now on anti-terrorist activities.

All throughout South America, military and para-military forces use dogs in the fight against major crime as well as in a traditional military working dog (MWD) patrol mode. Patrol dogs are used to track down guerrilla insurgents such as the Colombian FARC group, the same way tracker dogs were used in Vietnam four decades ago. In the fight against FARC, who at one point controlled up to 40 per cent of Colombia, military dogs have played a vital role.

Since 2001, the Colombian air force has strengthened resources in the use of dogs for security and defence of their air bases, to prevent terrorist acts that can cause irreparable damage to personnel, equipment, facilities and institutions. The air force has made strides towards improving and optimising MWD management. Currently Colombia is the only country in the world that has 2,800 dogs working in security. MWDs are trained in multiple techniques to counter the actions of terrorists. They have had excellent results; dogs have detected landmines and explosive devices, captured would-be terrorists and been involved in the confiscation of many shipments of drugs.

Recently 49 Belgian malinois dogs were trained in military specialties for air units. In the past five years, the Canine Training Centre Military (CICAM) has trained canines for the air force, army and navy, as well as the Administrative Security Department, the Technical Research unit, the National Penitentiary Institute and the Special Administrative Unit of Civil Aeronautics. Roles have included narcotics detection, explosives detection, foreign currency detection, search and rescue and perimeter patrol dogs.

The Head of Security and Defence of air bases, based on the evaluation of operational results, has recently purchased new dogs from the best European bloodlines. The Colombian Air Force, in coordination with the Mexican Association of Canine Rescue, exchanged knowledge in the development of search and rescue operations for victims of accidents or terrorist attacks. Likewise the Colombian military has provided training to Mexico on explosives and narcotics detection dogs. The CICAM is developing an ambitious project: advanced MWD training to enable a dog to alert on the presence of a narco-terrorist, sniper or a remote device operator at a great distances.

URUGUAY

In 1970 the 13th Armoured Infantry Battalion originally formed the cornerstone for training dogs of war. In 1998 they decided to develop several types of MWDs. This project involves the training of instructors and handlers, as well as breeding and dog training.

Today, Operations Group K-9 is the operative element of different specialty uses of MWDs in Uruguay. Well before the events of 11 September 2001, the army understood that terrorist threats or natural disasters would require search and rescue dogs to save lives. To this aim the Uruguayan National Army has spent considerable resources on this capability. Uruguay was one of the first countries to deploy search and rescue dog teams to Haiti after the 2010 earthquake. Explosives-detection teams support the operational ordnance equipment terrorists brigade (EDATE), mainly in safety inspections during visits to the country by foreign civilian and military authorities, as well as support for the presidency of the republic.

A team of highly specialised instructors from the US military are currently in Uruguay training military and police dogs for use in the detection of explosives: a new area of expertise for local law enforcement and armed forces. A total of eighteen dogs from the Uruguayan army, navy, air force and police are part of this training, which is specifically targeted at finding explosives in a variety of scenarios. Teams are trained in realistic settings, such as barracks, ships, passenger terminals, warehouses, vehicles, and aircraft. The project is part of an international effort to thwart the threat of terrorism.

Training for explosives detection is identical to training for drug detection—the only difference is the scent they are taught to recognise. Initially it involves a considerable amount of rapport building: the handler shows his dog plenty of love and trust buids up, advancing gradually into teaching the dog how to play with a toy for his reward. Dogs have a mental age equivalent to a three- or four-year-old child. Therefore a loud and childish tone of voice is used to praise his efforts. This is followed by repetition training. At first, the dogs are taught to detect about half a dozen types of explosives. The usual response is to sit in front of the detected target and wait for the reward. Once this routine is achieved, the dog can be trained to recognise additional scents and detect all types of explosives, in even the minutest quantities.

The Uruguayan dogs have been responding extremely well to the training. They include German shepherds, a pit bull, a Spanish setter and a mixed breed. The US instructors have so far been impressed with the quality of dogs in training In fact, they are considering Uruguay as a possible procurement source to purchase dogs for their own training within the US Department of Defense.

BRAZIL

In Brazil the Military Police (MP) are a preventive state police force responsible for maintaining public order within the states and the federal district; they are subordinate to the state government. The investigation of crime is handled by the civil police forces of the various states. Brazilian MP uses various breeds of dogs including German shepherds, malinois, Rottweilers, labradors and Bloodhounds.

The Brazilian army began to officially use MWDs in the 1960s. In 1967 the Brazilian army prepared a guide that authorised the use of dogs in military organisations, particularly for training courses, on operations in the jungle and with parachute teams. Currently, the Brazilian army uses working dogs at security points and sensitive areas, on vital escort tasks, guarding of prisoners and searching for drugs and explosives. Military dog handlers receive a 60-day training course on the theories of dealing with dogs, dog psychology, practices and techniques, veterinary care and the use of dogs in military activities.

The Brazilian army has branches all over the country and the units dealing with dogs are called *Secções de Cães-de-Guerra*. These units come under the responsibility of the Brazilian Army Logistics Department with its headquarters in Brasília. The Military Police are responsible for the breeding and selection of dogs within the Brazilian military. The Reproduction Centre for dogs-of-war is located in Brasília.

CHILE

For more than eight years the army of Chile has counted on the help of many different dogs in their units. The specific work of these dogs includes the detection of explosives and drugs, and search and rescue missions in the mountains. The majority of military dogs are labradors, golden retrievers and St Bernards. They are available for service in all parts of the country. In total there are thirty thirty dogs working in the army.

In the Military Police Regiment, located in Peñalolén, Santiago, dogs are utilised for the detection of explosives and all kinds of powders, such as TNT, C4 and TX. Drug-detection dogs are used to execute internal drug controls on soldiers. There are also small units of dogs, mainly St Bernards, in the mountain regiments throughout the country. These dogs are specifically trained in search and rescue operations in the harsh Andean regions of Chile.

ECUADOR

Ecuadorian canineunits of the 9th Special Forces Brigade Patria consists of paratroopers, many specialised as commandos, operational free jumpers, mountain warfare, frogmen, snipers and specialist military dog handlers. Today the Ecuadorian army maintains a military presence to control its borders with its neighbours, protecting against the entry of guerrilla groups and illegal migrations from Peru. The military also engages in anti-narcotics work from Peru and Colombia.

AUSTRALASIA

AUSTRALIA

It should be noted that Australian soldiers were using military working dogs (MWDs) as far back as World War I, but only when on attachments, such as Australian troops serving in British signal units. During World War II, Australian troops were supplied dogs to use in particular campaigns by Allied forces.

One such dog, Sandy, operated in the Faria Valley, New Guinea with the 2/27th Australian Infantry Battalion. Sandy was one of the many dogs trained by the United States Dog Detachment for the Australian Army and used as scouts and messengers during forward patrols.

The Australian Army as an entity began using patrol and tracker dogs as far back as the Korean War, the Malayan War, and in Borneo. Dog training was then conducted by members of the British Army's RAVC and British SAS units. The Royal Engineers trained mine detecting dogs in Korea. Four Royal Australian Regiments (RAR) in Borneo operated the tracker dogs Gunnar, Rank, Simba and Toddy. These dogs tracked and also acted as a reconnaissance element when required. In dense jungle the dogs could pick up the trail from the visual trackers and run in pursuit of the scent, often dragging the handlers around, through or over the massive buttress roots of gigantic trees. Disconcertingly, when enemy forces were not located the trackers' reports of these pursuits were often not believed. This unfortunately resulted in a misunderstanding of the dogs' true abilities. In hindsight we know now that the Indonesians, aware that the dogs were after them, escaped back over to their side of the border.

During the Vietnam War, the Australian Army provided two units of dogs trained by the Tracking Wing of the School of Infantry. When Australia's involvement in Vietnam ended the unit was disbanded.

The dog tracker teams in Vietnam, valuable targets for the Viet Cong, sadly could not be brought back with their handlers to the United States or Australia. Many stories about the dogs tell of the close attachments formed between animal and handler, and the anguish of soldiers when their time came to return to Australia. It was Australian Army policy that the dogs not be brought home at the end of their service, due to stringent quarantines.

The dogs were the core of combat tracker teams that were used from 1967 until the last combat troops left in late 1972. Trained from the age of about ten months at the Tracking Wing of the Ingleburn Infantry Centre, New South Wales, two dogs were assigned to each of the Australian battalions at the Task Force base at Nui Dat, in Phuoc Tuy Province. Full-time use of the dogs in Vietnam from late 1967 followed their successful use in Malaya in the 1950s and a trial in Vietnam during most of 1967.

Housed in kennels at Nui Dat, the dogs' lives followed an established routine. They were groomed and checked every day and taken outside the base perimeter for training runs on tracks set through the bush. South Vietnamese soldiers were usually used to set scent trails, so the dogs could get used to following their distinctive smell.

Eleven of the most popular contributors to the Australian war effort in Vietnam could not return home when their tour of duty ended. They were the six black labradors and five crossbreed tracker dogs used by the Australian Task Force. Each tracker team, consisting of the two dogs and their handlers, two visual trackers and two cover men (a machine-gunner and a signaller), operated on standby out of Nui Dat. Usually called out to follow up enemy trails or to locate suspected enemy hideouts after a contact, the teams would be airlifted by helicopter into the area of operation. The dogs loved these helicopter flights, finding the cool air a relief from the oppressive tropical heat. Once on the ground, the dog would be put on to the scent of the retreating enemy. The dog would follow the scent, usually at speed, until a location was found, when he would stop with nose extended facing the suspected hideout. The tracker and dog would then fall back while the rest of the section searched the area, often finding wounded enemies or recently occupied bunker systems that would have otherwise been missed.

The dogs were outstandingly successful at their combat tasks in Vietnam. Apart from their success in locating enemies and their support systems, the dogs saved the lives of their handlers and team members on many occasions. Although not trained to detect mines (despite recommendations by some soldiers that mine dogs be used in Vietnam), the dogs were intelligent and sufficiently well-trained to do so. Some dogs, according to their handlers, could detect the wind breeze over a trip wire and indicate its presence.

The first Army Police Dog section was formed in 1977. The purpose of this unit was to maintain a high level of security for the Army Aviation Centre in Queensland, a role which remains to this day. It was known as the Base Support Squadron Police Dog Unit and boasted a posted strength of five dog teams. The members were all volunteers and came from various corps.

MWDs underwent many changes over the next decade including several name changes. Members were still recruited from all corps and retained whatever pay level they had previously been allocated. In 1990 the unit was given a singular identity when they were incorporated into the Royal Australian Corps of Military Police (RACMP). Incorporation into the RACMP provided for all members to receive the same pay level, and opened up both career progression and posting opportunities. Today they are called the MP Dog Platoon, Delta Company 1 MP Battalion.

The next major change to occur was the introduction of new training doctrine, which saw the phasing out of police dog training, and the commencement of MWD training.

The current peacetime tasks of the unit are to provide:
• specialist information unit commanders
• discipline and morale within the Army Aviation Centre;
• maintenance of law and order
• vital asset protection/key point security (i.e. aircraft, airfields, defence installations, etc.)

- prevention of unauthorised removal of classified material
- defence aid to the civil community and agencies
- defence force aid to the civil power
- search and rescue capability
- VIP protection
- security of visiting forces' aircraft

The war time role incorporates all of the aforementioned responsibilities, with added responsibilities including the following:

- early warning at checkpoints
- building searches
- movement and detention of prisoners of war
- special operations
- support to Australian Defence Forces (ADF), (infantry assisting with listening posts, clearing patrols and the pursuit of fleeing enemy)

Operation Astute is the Australian government's response to a request from the government of Timor-Leste to assist in restoring peace to their country. The ADF has deployed to Timor-Leste to assist the government and the United Nations to bring stability, security and confidence to the Timorese. There are approximately 1,000 ADF personnel currently serving in Timor-Leste.

Police from Australia and 24 other nations throughout the world provide security in the capital, Dili. The ADF provides support to these police operations as required. Military Police (MP) MWD teams are at the forefront of these support operations; the local population has learnt to respect these canine soldiers.

MP dogs are not the only military dogs in the Australian Army. The Royal Australian Engineers (RAE) use explosive detection dogs (EDD). Today, EDDs are used in a specialist search capacity to counter the threat of improvised explosive devices (IEDs) throughout Oruzgan Province in Afghanistan within the Reconstruction Task Force. Long before the recent upsurge in terrorism throughout the world, military units have relied on dogs for their innate scenting abilities. This has included the safe and accurate method of detecting explosives: a fact of life in military environments.

The army engineers operated a mine detection dog program as far back as 1952, when Australians operated British-trained MDDs during the Korean War. In 1953 the School of Military Engineering (SME) began training dogs for both guarding and mine detection. As in several other Commonwealth countries, the Australian dogs were trained using British army doctrine. With the passage of time the infantry took over the tracker dogs and the Royal Australian Air Force (RAAF) took over the training of guard dogs. The call for mine dogs diminished with the cessation of the Malayan War, so the mine dogs section at SME terminated in 1959.

In 1970 the army decided to reintroduce mine and explosive detecting dogs in response to growing combat casualty lists caused by mines and IEDs in the Vietnam War. In that same year Captain George Hulse was selected to attend the Mine and Tunnel Dog Course at Fort Benning, Georgia, USA. Although he trained dogs upon his return, Australia's involvement in that war ceased in 1972 and the dogs were not sent. In 1981 the wing changed its name to the Explosive Detection Dog Wing due the fact that Australia was a signatory to the UN Banned Mines resolution and the word 'mine' was thought to be inappropriate.

Today army EDD teams use passive detection response off-lead detection dogs. They are of several breeds including mixed breeds; many are sourced from animal shelters. The primary role today is deployment overseas on ADF operations. In the event of enactment of the Defence Aid to Civil Community (DACC) Federal legislation, EDD teams can be used in the public sector. In the past this has included assistance to the 2000 Olympics, 2002 Commonwealth Heads of State Meeting (CHOGM) and 2003 Rugby World Cup.

Some recent operations using dog teams were Operation Anode to the Solomon Islands, where twelve EDD teams rotated in-country over a twelve-month period in support of the Australian Federal Police (AFP). Dogs were deployed to Somalia as part of the UN, East Timor, Bougainville and today to operations in Afghanistan. The Combat Engineers Regiment (CER) are used extensively within Afghanistan during search operations in villages for arms hides, detection of IEDs and at vehicle checkpoints.

The Australian contribution to ISAF in Afghanistan has focused on the Special Forces fight against the Taliban within Uruzgan and North Helmand provinces. However a 440-man Mentoring and Reconstruction Task Force (MRTF) has been very active in southern Afghanistan, not only rebuilding structure but also training the army and police forces. Within this group the Australian engineers have deployed EDD teams.

EDDs are a key tool in locating insurgent IEDs and weapons caches. Recently Australia's engineers worked to rebuild a bridge on Afghanistan's Highway 1, which had been destroyed by insurgent explosives. The four-day operation was concentrated on conducting searches of local compounds. These searches yielded several caches of explosives and ammunition, thanks to the EDD team. The caches were searched and their contents destroyed in an explosion controlled by Australian engineers.

Australian military working dogs served under the United Nations' flag in Sinai, Cambodia, Bougainville, Kosovo and East Timor. Current operations include EDD teams in Afghanistan and, recently, Military Police in Timor Leste. Today Australia's combined military services use more MWDs than at any time in its history.

Australia sent three EDDs from 3 Combat Engineer Regiment to UNSOM Operations Baidoa, Somalia in 1993. Dogs were often watched by large crowds of Somalis; many of the African races fear dogs and they prove a great force multiplier. All three dogs sent to Somalia returned to Australia under closely supervised quarantine regulations.

Other Operators

As a result of a fire at Naval Air Station (NAS) Nowra in December 1976, which completely destroyed a hangar and numerous Tracker aircraft, the Royal Australian Navy (RAN) saw the need to upgrade security. In early 1977 police dogs were introduced to that station. Initially, dogs and handlers from the RAAF were used. The first naval police and police dog team took up duties in July 1979.

Within Australian government departments are several agencies that use dogs in the fight against terrorism and major crime. In Australia the

Customs Department protects borders with specialist detection dogs; likewise quarantine requirements are aided by the beagle brigade. The country's state, territory and federal police forces operate general duties and specialist detection dogs. Finally, many corrective services use guard and specialist dogs.

Royal Australian Air Force (RAAF)

Dogs were first introduced into the RAAF during 1943, when untrained and extremely savage dogs were let loose inside warehouses and compounds, tied to aircraft or fixed to long lines in such a manner that they could run back and forth. Later patrol dogs were used by the RAAF security guards to guard vital assets of a base.

Traditionally the RAAF employed police dogs for the sole purpose of security. While this type of dog could track using 'wind' scent, it was generally aggressive to strangers, and predominantly used on lone foot patrols on the flight line. While reasonably effective in a benign security environment, these dogs were not considered suitable for use in ground defence operations. In 1996 a project team was formed to assess the capability of MWDs working with Air Defence Guards in the patrol and surveillance area (PSA), close approach area (CAA) and close defence area (CDA).

In 1994 police dog handler mustering underwent a further change and became incorporated into the RAAF police mustering. In 1997 dog handlers, police and police investigators were mustered under RAAF security police.

With the advent of modern warfare, the role of the dog handler changed to reflect the dog's specialist capability in a new security role. Belgian malinois and German shepherds were the breeds of choice and their training gives the RAAF the benefit of having man and dog security teams capable of seeking out an enemy before he can damage vital assets. Advanced tracking, combat troop support, tarmac protection and booby trap detection are all part of the MWD's duties. With the capability of working in all terrains, from heavy scrub to urban areas, these dogs and the new breed of handlers led the Australian Defence Forces into the new millennium.

The RAAF security police work with MWDs to provide security at RAAF bases. The two breeds of dog currently used are the German shepherd and the Belgian malinois. The dogs and their handlers are trained by the Military Working Dog Training Flight at Amberley. Their working environments can vary, from modern air bases located near state capital cities, to bare bases located in remote regions of Australia. During their careers, the MWD handlers and their dogs could also be deployed to foreign locations, such as Solomon Islands, the Middle East and East Timor.

MWDs are now a well-established force multiplier within the Australian Defence Force (ADF). The RAAF are the recognised ADF leaders in the field of operating MWDs. RAAF MWD roles are now varied and encompass policing and security functions as well as advanced tracker skills used operationally overseas.

Far from decreasing in numbers in the age of advanced technology MWDs are on the increase in all major military powers. Over recent years coalition forces have dramatically increased their use of MWDs in the fight against terrorism. EDDs are in particularly high demand and the RAAF established their own EDD teams separate from the Australian army for use around bases. Regardless of modern technology, MWDs are still the best way to patrol forward operational bases, particularly at night and at vehicle checkpoints.

The RAAF also maintains several MWD handlers attached to the Air Field Defence Wing. The Airfield Defence Guards (ADGs) are an elite specialist Infantry-type formation on the same lines as the British RAF Regiment. These MWDs are used in the traditional Infantry patrol role, scouting ahead of a section of ADGs. RAAF MWD teams have led Australian Army Infantry patrols in East Timor and some members are currently operational with Australia's Special Air Service in undisclosed locations.

Today, the RAAF is the largest single corporate user of MWDs in Australia. Its approximate 200 MWDs have an important role in the security of high-value RAAF assets at twelve bases and establishments located across Australia. The RAAF currently has several trained dog handlers on international active duty. The RAAF negotiated with a protocol

AQIS (Australian Quarantine and Inspection Service) that allows MWDs to re-enter Australia with only one month of quarantine. After quarantine, these MWDs are returned to their units in the Army and RAAF for further military duty.

New Zealand

'Cry Havoc' was the unofficial motto of the Royal New Zealand Air Force (RNZAF) Police Dog Section, displayed on all badges and plaques of the unit. The Dog Unit was first established in 1967 when the RNZAF first purchased the P3 Orion Aircraft from the United States. Due to the sensitive nature of the electronic equipment on board these aircraft, it was stipulated that additional security measures had to be put in place to prevent unauthorised access. Dogs were chosen primarily for their vastly superior sense of smell, sharpness of hearing and a visual ability to detect even the smallest of movements. The dogs could work in a variety of conditions and would reduce the manpower required for this task. Thus the RNZAF Police Dog Unit was established and built at its current location adjacent to the main gate at Base Auckland, Whenuapai airfield.

At that time the RNZAF Police Dog Section (RNZAFPDS) was a sub-unit of the RNZAF Police Corps, the only Corps uniquely within the RNZAF. All candidates were qualified RNZAF policemen in the general duties branch before becoming dog handlers. Candidates could also be selected from the RNZMP and Naval Regulating Branch.

Role

The role of the (RNZAFPDS) is to provide security to air force aircraft, sensitive facilities, VIPs and tri-service support.

The RNZAF maintains the only canine unit within the New Zealand Defence Force. As such all members were capable of working in the field alongside Army units, and dog handlers receive regular weapons and Infantry core training. In particular, close cooperation has developed between the Royal New Zealand Military Police (RNZMP) using EDD search teams and MWD teams for close personnel protection, residential security details, the New Zealand Infantry and New Zealand Special Air Service (NZSAS). The last unit utilises the dog section during escape and evasion training. To this end, a large part of the general police dog course is devoted to tracking in various terrains, not just that found within the confines of an air base. One unique aspect unique is visual tracker training, which was taught initially by the ex-Royal Army Vet Corps (RAVC) instructors and became part of the dog course during the tracking phase.

The New Zealand Army did use dogs under the direction of the British army in the 1963 Malaysian War. New Zealand Special Air Service (NZSAS) Troopers were trained by Royal Army Veterinary Corps (RAVC) dog instructors. The British used a two-tier system to combat the enemy. The first element of the plan required relocating the inhabitants of smaller hamlets into a larger village. Small British units would live with the villagers, providing medical and other assistance while protecting them from communist insurgents. This part of the program was dubbed 'hearts and minds'. The second element of the defence strategy involved reconnaissance or hunter-killer teams. Each ten-man team was composed of two identical sub-teams, made up of a team leader, a visual tracker, a radio operator, a cover man and a dog handler with a trained labrador retriever. These teams took the war to the enemy wherever he was hiding. The units were also known as Combat Tracker Teams (CTTs).

In the 1980s there were several specialist dog teams in the RNZAF: EDDs and narcotic detection dogs (NDDs). The former are used within the RNZAF and RNZMP for searching at vehicle checkpoints, VIP transport, aircraft facilities and during CPP operations. These dogs have found a full range of explosives and firearms. They have been used frequently by the civilian authorities to search international airports and during other IED emergencies around the country. All qualified RNZAF specialist detection dogs were trained a second time by the NZ Civilian Police Service; this negated any legal issues in relation to presentation of evidence in civilian courts.

EDD operations, as in the Australian Defence Force (ADF), were firstly considered to be best used by the Corps of Engineers. However, since the

RNZAF are the only animal operators within New Zealand defence it was sensibly decided to place them under RNZAFP control.

Due to their tri-service employment, narcotic specialist search dogs were trained to work aboard ships and planes and exposed to battlefield conditions. These handlers worked regularly with the RNZMP and Naval Regulating Branch. The NDDs were used in the garrison policing role and were an effective deterrent during random vehicle and barrack searches. NDD operations were conducted covertly, usually in conjunction with Service Investigation Branch (SIB) operations with command directly from the Provost Marshall's Office.

As the NDD section was located at an air force base they were constantly used for passenger and cargo screening, usually tasked alongside or on behalf of the Customs Department. Again, NDD were thus trained by the police, who also qualified all Customs Department handlers in New Zealand to ensure continuity of court evidence and standards.

Dog School

The RNZAF Police Dog School has trained many other agencies, their personnel or dogs in general duties and specialist dog roles. These include the New Zealand Police, Customs, Aviation Security, Corrective Services, Civil Defence and Red Cross Society (the latter two departments in the use of search and rescue dogs). The RNZAF Police Dog School has also trained personnel and exported trained dogs to the armed forces of Singapore, Fiji and the Sultan of Brunei.

Dogs

RNZAF police dogs are obtained through donations from the public. Dogs are usually male (the exception being a female German shepherd explosive detection dog in the early 1990s), are around eighteen months of age and are purebred German shepherds. Specialist search dogs were male black labradors.

RNZAF police dogs are teamed with one handler only for their operational life. Dogs live at home with their handlers and will retire after a minimum of seven years of operational use, when the dogs are given to the handler. If a handler, on the other hand, departs service prior to the police dog reaching five years of age it is the general practice to re-team the dog with another handler.

Transport

Transport is provided by way of four-by-four Landrovers or four-by-four Toyota Hiluxes. The vehicles are specially fitted out with air conditioning, non-slip floors, vents, equipment storage and dividing cages for multiple dog use. The alterations usually cost half as much again as the initial government purchase price of the vehicle. However, vehicles are only to get teams to their destination and to respond to incidents. A working police dog's abilities cannot be best utilised at speed in the comfort of a patrol car, so IRPCs (Individual Rubber Personnel Carriers—boots to most of us!) are the main form of transport. Most handlers would walk in excess of 10 kilometres (6 miles) per shift. The dogs are also familiarised with helicopter and aircraft flights in case of operational requirements.

The RNZAF Dog Section's first officer in command was an ex-warrant officer in the RAVC, and he can be credited with laying down the unit's modus operandi. An example of this is the idea of not letting old skills disappear. Some general duties dogs were trained to detect mines, some were trained to carry packs or to conduct cadaver search. The idea is to retain these skills in case they are required again in future conflicts. Thus, dog handlers in the RNZAF were encouraged to seek additional knowledge in their chosen career. Several staff trained as vet technicians, or in zoology, while others worked part-time as animal welfare officers, dog breeders and lecturers on wild canid history and behaviour. One member went overseas at their own expense to learn husky sled training in Canada.

The net result of all this was every RNZAF dog handler was capable of establishing a dog unit or training dogs to an operational level if required. This again is a reflection of the influence the RAVC's foundations had on the unit's outlook.

Training

Training for general duties dogs is held over an intensive thirteen-week course; not all dogs or handlers will pass this physically and mentally demanding requirement. There are always more applicants than positions, and some candidates have to wait several years before an opening becomes available. Prior to course commencement, the suitability of hopeful candidates is evaluated over a week.

After the initial thirteen weeks of training, dog handlers work for several years patrolling military establishments. Handlers also conduct continuation training once a week for four hours, which all have to attend regardless of shift work. Additionally, dog demonstrations are conducted for the public; some events, such as military tattoos, are viewed by thousands of people. This all takes time to practice and thus adds to an operational team's workload. Specialist dog teams attend continuation training with the civilian police and Customs Department at their centres to retain skills and qualifications in those fields.

The RNZAFPDS was a relatively small unit (twelve members) but, due to its enthusiastic and professional staff, was highly effective. It crammed a great deal of diversity and operational ability into a small team, resulting in successes usually requiring a much larger force. In the late 1980s, ground combat training was commenced, which eventually turned into the basis for the Air Security Guard mustering of 2000. The concept increased the security and combat readiness of the RNZAF.

In 2000 the RNZAF Police Dog Section, as part of the RNZAF Police ceased to exist and was re-formed as part of the new RNZAF Air Security Guard mustering. Over the years the Dog Unit has managed to survive many changes in its role and focus, as well as command and management. Numbers of handlers declined at one stage down to only one. In 2003 the RNZAF deployed dogs, in support of Operation Rata, to the Solomon Islands. This was the first time RNZAF MWDs were deployed overseas in an operational role. Between 2003 and 2004 a total of three dog teams were deployed on Solomon operations, where they were to prove their worth as a force multiplier, protecting RNZAF assets on the ground.

Now, under the Expeditionary Support Squadron (ESS) umbrella, the Dog Unit maintains a focus on operational readiness to support the force element groups. This includes the provision of security at RNZAF Bases and deployments within New Zealand.

AFRICA

Military working dogs (MWDs) were used in Africa by Colonial powers from the early years of that continent's settlement by Europeans. British, French, German and Belgian military forces all used dogs for sentry and guard work. This proved a useful force multiplier in those days as many natives were afraid of these European animals, which were trained to bark and bite the locals. It appears that apart from the Republic of South Africa, many African nations do not use MWDs in great numbers. This may be partially due to their general distrust of dogs, religious beliefs or cultural attitudes.

There are, of course, still MWDs operating throughout the continent, usually employed by United Nations forces. The French use them in base security roles in their African protectorates. In Somalia in 1993, MWDs were used by several UN Forces in the explosive detection dog (EDD) role.

RHODESIA

Even though no longer a country in name, Rhodesia is worth a mention due to its early successful use of MWDs.

The Rhodesian army developed several innovative tactical employments of MWDs using airpower. One example was the use of long-range dog handling. Early in the Rhodesian Bush War, when security forces were often tracking one or two guerrillas, tracking dogs were used to hunt them down. To increase their range and mobility, security forces outfitted tracking dogs with harnesses carrying two-way radios and an orange panel. The dog's handler would then watch the dog from a helicopter, which also held a team of soldiers. By listening to the dog's breathing and heartbeats, the handler could follow the hunt, giving commands by radio as needed. Once the dog had cornered its quarry, the soldiers on board the helicopter would deal with the insurgents. This tactic was successful early in the war before insurgent bands became larger. The Rhodesian army also employed MWDs in the 5th Engineer Support Squadron.

The role of the 5th Engineer Dog Troop was to train all mine dogs and handlers up to the standard required for deployment on operations. They also provided continuation training for all dogs and dog handlers and provided mine dog teams for operational tasks.

KENYA

Kenya has a history of using MWDs dating back to British colonial times, when members of the Royal Army Veterinary Corps (RAVC) used tracker dogs to hunt down Mau Mau terrorists. Since independence, a small force of dogs have been used by the Armed Forces Constabulary in the guard role. Kenya's MWD mission is to provide physical security to armed forces installation and protect them from theft or damage. They do this by the provision of physical security to armed forces installations. They are responsible for the breeding, training and upkeep of guard dogs within the defence force.

REPUBLIC OF SOUTH AFRICA

In the 1980s the South African Army had various specialist units in the fight against terrorist groups. One of these was South West African Specialist Unit (SWASPES). Based at Otavi, the Koevoet Dog section within this unit was an elite counter insurgency team (COIN) deployed to combat the terrorist threat from 1979 to 1989. Today, within the South African Army, dog squads exist in specialist infantry units

The South African Medical Service (SAMS) was established as a full service branch of the SADF in 1979 to consolidate the medical services of all three services. They provide comprehensive medical care for military personnel and their dependents, as well as the police and employees of other security-related government departments. The SAMS provides veterinary services for animals (mainly horses and dogs) used by the military.

THE FUTURE OF WAR DOGS

The future looks bright for military working dogs (MWDs); there is no sign of any modern technology being developed anytime soon that will be able to cost-effectively detect an offender or particular odour day or night in various environments and do something about it via indication or physical action. If anything, we have yet to see the full potential of MWDs being developed.

The future canine warrior, like his human counterpart, may look like a science fiction figure with advanced protective body armour, all-terrain boots, eye protection goggles, attached optical vision and acoustic aids to allow the handler to see what his canine partner can and be able to communication giving commands at a distance, advanced supplements or medications to enhance performance, a breathing system enabling the dog to work in contaminated environments and anything else our imaginations could conceive.

In fact, military working dog equipment has gone full circle several times in their history in warfare. We have seen war dogs bred and selected for their large size, equipped with leather spiked collars or clad in metal body armour. In World War I, dogs were issued gas masks for protection but generally wore no equipment as they needed to speedily carry messages from the front to the rear Headquarters. In modern times, partially due to technology and partly due to MWDs being recognised as a valued and expensive piece of kit, MWD are seen wearing lightweight body armour, foot protection, eye protection and other items to enhance their performance on the battle field.

Gone are the days of World War I where white dogs were painted black so not to stand out; dogs are now bred for camouflaging colours. There has even been research into the genetic possibility of breeding the perfect MWD who has all the scenting, fitness, silence, aggression and colour traits needed in a war dog.

Recent deployments by both the British and United States Forces in Iraq and Afghanistan have showed the need for better cooperation and joint training between MWD units. Manpower is a factor: simply put, there are not enough MWDs or personnel within the US army to cope with the mission objectives. Therefore the US army were required to supplement their MWD teams with counterparts from the USAF Marines and Navy. Fortunately for the United States, the USAF Security Police do undertake extensive ground combat training as their role also includes Airfield Defence.

Similarly, in the British forces, the Royal Air Force Police (RAFP) have had to fill major shortfalls within the British defence capability by deploying alongside their army counterparts. The RAFP operates a large police dog section, with detachments at many RAF stations.

Both the UK and USA have established defence training schools where dogs from all services are trained. In Australia and New Zealand, both Air Forces are the lead agencies in training all service MWDs. Likewise, throughout Europe many countries operate tri-service dog schools, mainly for economic reasons. In short, it's important to use the resources available to better fulfil the mission tasked to us. As the British and Americans have established by using existing tri-service MWD assets, it is a far better option than temporary recruitment increases. The key is to ensure all MWD teams can perform core skills that are interchangeable with all services, thus optimising manpower.

In the United Kingdom a new regiment of MWDs was created in 26 March 2010. The surge in operational demand for MWDs in recent years has seen five independent units formed 101, 102, 103, 104 and 105 MWD Support Units have supported operations in Bosnia, Kosovo, Northern Ireland, Iraq and Afghanistan from their respective bases in Aldershot, North Luffenham in the United Kingdom and Sennelager in Germany.

The regiment will consist of 284 soldiers and officers and about 200 MWDs and will continue to be based in three locations in the UK and Germany. Its primary operational role is the support of the lead brigade in Afghanistan with the provision of protection and specialist military working dogs and veterinary support to the command.

General Officer Commanding Theatre Troops, Major General Bruce Brealey has taken a personal interest in the formation of the Regiment. He said: 'The formation of first Military Working Dog Regiment is a major step forward in the development of a key capability that is making a major contribution to operational success every day in Afghanistan.'

The commanding officer of Military Working Dog Regiment Lt Col David Thorpe said 'military working dogs have been in the vanguard of recent and on-going operations in Iraq and Afghanistan and are a key force multiplier across the full spectrum of operations. The formation of the regiment is a further step forward in generating, optimising and sustaining military working dog capability. The energy and enthusiasm of the dogs is matched equally by the dedication, care and skill of the dog handlers, support team and veterinary staff. Together, they bring a unique capability to the battlefield making sure that our troops can find, avoid or dispose of improvised explosive devices.'

Let us not forget these unsung heroes are soldiers, too. These valiant dogs protect our military men and women through countless perils, give comfort in uncertainty, and share the suffering and the risks in the time of war. Over the decades, many of these dogs have made the supreme sacrifice, giving their own lives to shield our armed forces and military assets from hostile acts. Canines in the armed forces continue that noble tradition around the world today.

SOURCES

BOOKS

Cooper, Jilly, 1983. *Animals in War*. Heinemann, London
Dean, Charles L., 2005. Soldiers and Sled Dogs. University of Nebraska Press, USA
Grambo, Rebecca L., 2005. *Wolf: Legend, Enemy, Icon*. Firefly Books, USA
Hammer, Blythe, 2006. *Dogs at War*. Carlton Books, London
Hill, Anthony, 2005. *Animal Heroes*. Penguin Australia, Melbourne

PERIODICALS

Australian & NZ Defender Magazine
Australian Working Dog Magazine
Magazine of the Royal Army Veterinary Corps

WEBSITES

home.iprimus.com.au/buckomp
http://rafpolicehistory.blogspot.com
www. british.gov.defence.com
www.47ipsd.us
www.af.mil
www.anzacday.org.au
www.army.mil
www.armydogunit-ni.co.uk
www.aussietrackers.tripod.com
www.bmlv.gv.at
www.cbp.gov
www.combattrackerteam.org
www.community-2.webtv.net
www.defence.gov.au

www.defense.gouv.fr
www.defense.gov
www.forsvaret.dk
www.fortunecity.com
www.he.admin.ch
www.isayeret.com
www.lackland.af.mil
www.legion-etrangere.com
www.marines.mil
www.mil.be
www.militaryphotos.net
www.militaryworkingdogs.com
www.navy.mil
www.nwdm.org
www.olive-drab.com
www.oneijak.com
www.palacebarracksmemorialgarden.org
www.qmfound.com
www.streitkraeftebasis.de
www.uswardogs.org
www.war-dogs.com
www.wikipedia.org
www.wood.army.mil
www.zahal.org

GOVERNMENT STAFF AND DEPARTMENTS

Aspirant Chalmeau Department Gendarmerie Service historique de la Defence
Asta Galdikait, Public Relations Department, Ministry of Defence Republic of Lithuania
Balint Nagy, Consul-General of Hungary.
Brigadier Babar Mansoor Virk, Defence Advisor High Commission of Pakistan
Capt Jatinder Singh, Indian Navy Defence Adviser, High Commission of India
Captain Fedja Vranicar, Public Relations Officer, Slovakia MOD
Carlo Schijvenaars, Public Affairs Officer, Woensdrecht Airbase
Christoph Görgen, specialist subject teacher at the Bundeswehr School of Dog handling.
Christoph Görgen, The Bundeswehr School of Dog handling
Colonel Mario Tassini, Italian Defence Attaché
Colonel Mauricio Araya, Defence Attaché of Chile
CPO (Navy) Diego Hernandez, Defence Attaché Assistant Embassy of Spain
Department of the Air Force, 341st Training Squadron
Directorate of History and Heritage, Canadian Defence Nationale.

Ewa Walczuk, Information Officer, Embassy of Finland

Jorge Gerando Parra Martinez, Esculela Cinologica de la Defensa

Lee Fad Ley, Malaysia Military Dog School

Lt Col (Australian Army) SO1, Malaysia Australia Joint Defence Program HQ, Malaysian Armed Forces, Kuala Lumpur

Lt Gen Delfin N Bangit, AFP Commanding General, Philippine Army

Marleah L Miller, USAF Community Relations

Mick Martin, NZAP 1722 Chapter 3 RNZAF Police Dogs

Militaire Kennels Commando en Kennel Centrum

Peter Söderberg Höghult Lövåsen, 2 S-546 95 Karlsborg

Ploenpit Meemeskul, Charge d Affairs, Royal Thai Embassy

Public Relations and Information Department, Ministry of Defence of the Republic of Croatia

Russian Department of Defence, Moscow

Ryszard Jeleniewicz, Chief of the Veterinary Corps of the Polish Armed Forces

Seda Besen, DA Office Manager Australian Embassy Ankara

SSG Yuen Tat Hoong Paravet, SAF Military Police Command Military Working Dog Unit

Stephen Dent, Australian Defence Force

Uldis Barkans, Major, Chief of the Dog Handler's Service of the State Border Guard College

About the Author

Nigel Allsopp started his military career in 1980 as a military working dog handler in the Royal New Zealand Air Force Police. Within his 15 years of service he rose to the rank of Dogmaster, responsible for all aspects of canine operations and training within the New Zealand Defence Force. During his service he was a military working dog handler, a specialist narcotic detection dog handler and an explosive detection handler at various times. He became the first military dog trainer to qualify as a NZ civilian police dog trainer and supervisor. Nigel has trained numerous government agencies, both in Australia and abroad, in the use of specialist dogs.

Nigel left the military to pursue a keen interest in wild canine research and worked as a trainer for the Auckland Zoo. He has written several articles on the behavioural enrichment of captive animals for international zoological journals. In Australia, he continued to pursue his interest in wild canines by at several zoos and wildlife parks. The desire to work with dogs again led Nigel to join the Queensland Police Service, where he is currently a Senior Constable in the QPS Dog Section.

Nigel is a member of the Australian Tracker and War Dog Association. He has written several articles on canine training for international law enforcement magazines and is a regular contributing author for the *Royal Army Veterinary Corps Journal*. Nigel is a vocal ambassador for the establishment of animal memorials to recognise their role in and contribution to war.

First published in 2011 by
New Holland Publishers (Australia) Pty Ltd

Sydney • Auckland • London • Cape Town

1/66 Gibbes Street Chatswood NSW 2067 Australia
218 Lake Road Northcote Auckland New Zealand
86 Edgware Road LondonW2 2EA United Kingdom
80 McKenzie Street Cape Town 8001 South Africa

National Library of Australia Cataloguing-in-Publication data:

Cry havoc / Nigel Allsop.

ISBN: 9781742570969 (pbk.)

Dogs--War use.
Working dogs

355.424

Publisher: Diane Jardine
Publishing manager: Lliane Clarke
Project editor: Talina McKenzie
Proofreader: Meryl Potter
Designer: Celeste Vlok
Production manager: Olga Dementiev
Printer: Ligare Book Printing Australia